Rolland and I have been deeply impacted by the ministry of Fred and Sharon Wright. After receiving prayer from them, my life was forever transformed. I am eternally thankful to them, and now they have written a beautiful book on thanksgiving! Having known this man and woman for nearly two decades, filled with Father God's love, it is with great joy that I recommend this book to you, not only to read but also to put into practice the giving of thanks with all that is within you! Read and be blessed.

— Heidi Baker
FOUNDING DIRECTOR, IRIS GLOBAL, MOZAMBIQUE

"THANK YOU, LORD!" How basic a concept, yet, how delightfully refreshing and renewing is this very important reminder to practise thanksgiving to God as a way of life. Read in a single sitting, I chuckled, nodded, reflected, smiled and even winced a time or two as the impact of Fred and Sharon's offering found its mark. Most remarkable is the progressively re-heightened sense of thanksgiving to God that is almost certain to well up in the heart of the reader, as it did in me. This transparent telling of experience and story interwoven with timeless scriptural truths serves as a timely catalyst to the more frequent and intentional thanksgiving that so needs to be a daily practice.

—Brenda C. Huger Hazel
FOUNDING & SENIOR PASTOR, LATTER RAIN CHRISTIAN FELLOWSHIP, NEW YORK

Certain topics of vital importance for the Christian walk can hold little appeal for believers who are drawn to subjects that seem more supernatural or exciting. Thanksgiving is often one of those. This small book, however, is filled with rich teaching of great benefit to beginners and mature believers alike. Refreshingly told, it's an easy read certain to lift your spirit and perhaps even spark a needed attitude adjustment. You will be blessed as you read!

—Loren Sandford
PASTOR OF NEW SONG CHURCH, COLORADO, AND AUTHOR OF SEVERAL BOOKS INCLUDING *Visions of the Coming Days* AND *Purifying The Prophetic*

Fred and Sharon Wright have been a spiritual father and mother to us and many others in the body of Christ. As the Founding Coordinators of Partners in Harvest, they have hungered for and pointed many others toward revival. Fred has always had a heart to sense the Holy Spirit's current edge, and his latest book on thanksgiving is a timely word to the body of Christ.

—Dan & Gwen Slade

INTERNATIONAL COORDINATORS, PARTNERS IN HARVEST

I am very happy to endorse a book on thanksgiving. I do not doubt the power of a life of thankfulness, nor the need to continually desire an increased understanding of the biblical foundations and truths related to it. Reading this book will be your invitation into the greater things of God through the pathway of thanks. It is a pathway that has been well-trodden throughout the years, but it is still as inviting and necessary as it was when King David first wrote what we now know as Psalm 100: *"Enter His gates with thanksgiving."*

—Paul Manwaring

GLOBAL LEGACY DIRECTOR, BETHEL CHURCH, REDDING, CALIFORNIA

THE POWER OF THANKSGIVING

The Power of Thanksgiving
Published by Catch The Fire Books
272 Attwell Drive, Toronto ON M9W 6M3 Canada

Distributed worldwide by Catch The Fire Distribution. Titles may be purchased in bulk. For information, please contact distribution@catchthefire.com.

Catch The Fire® is a registered trademark of Catch The Fire World.

ISBN 978-1-894310-34-5
Copyright © 2013 Fred and Sharon Wright

The Team: Emily Wright, Rachel McDonagh, Naomi Parnell, Benjamin Jackson, Jon Long, Jonathan Puddle, Steve Long.
Cover design: Emily Wright (Catch The Fire)
Layout design: Marcott Bernarde (Catch The Fire)

Printed in Canada
First Edition 2013

THE POWER OF
THANKSGIVING

FRED & SHARON WRIGHT

Once again, I dedicate this book to my wife of forty-eight years, Sharon.

She is once again my co-author. Without her partnership in marriage and her help with writing, this book would not have happened.

Many of the words are her words, but after our forty-eight years of becoming one flesh, it is hard for me to even recognize which are my words and which words are hers.

CONTENTS

FOREWORD

The Power of Thanksgiving is a timely and important book combating our continual propensity to complain and emphasize the few things that may be going wrong, over and against the multiplicity of things that are right and for which we must be thankful. I stopped short in my complaining, of being too busy and away too much etc. and began compiling a long list, thanking God for everything I could think of, including safe air travel, wonderful beds to sleep on, a hot shower in the morning, three meals per day, and especially for my wife who loves me; not to mention my children and the good health that I am enjoying. "THANK YOU, JESUS!" I am well aware that people today can be negative 80 percent of the time, and although I think this is totally unacceptable for Christians who have so much to be thankful for, I find myself falling back into that pattern altogether too frequently.

Why not let Fred and Sharon help you turn this around, as I have chosen to do. It will change your disposition, your family and relationships, and more importantly, you will find your joy and peace have returned. There is a reason that the Scripture says, *"In everything give thanks, for this is the will of God ..."* 1 Thessalonians 5:18.

Fred and Sharon have walked through more than their fair share of trials and difficulties in life. The death of a newborn baby, their struggles in ministry, down to their own health issues of cancer, stroke and seizure, yet they have come through it all praising God. If you persist in clinging to your right to complain, I can hear them both saying to you, "Try thanksgiving for 30 days and see how well it works, It has made all the difference for us!"

Be aware though, old patterns can be hard to break, so be determined and do this, set your face like a flint against negativity. You and yours will be so glad you did!

John Arnott
PRESIDENT AND FOUNDING PASTOR,
CATCH THE FIRE, TORONTO

ACKNOWLEDGMENTS

No book is written and released to the public by the author alone. Sharon and I acknowledge that freely as we finish up this booklet, *The Power of Thanksgiving.* This work was inspired first of all by a dream from God. Without his reminder of the importance of thanksgiving in his economy I would still be wandering a bit off track, through the maze of distractions with which life in a fallen world is filled! How grateful I am to him for his continual input into my life. I acknowledge his inspiration for this booklet and my utter dependence upon him for the adventure I have had with him during my lifetime.

I would also like to acknowledge my gratitude for all the training that my mother and father did to etch into me the importance of thanking God first of all for his provision, and then for the importance as a child after each Christmas and each birthday to acknowledge the gifts given to me and to express my thankfulness for their thoughtfulness.

On the practical side of getting this booklet to publication, I am grateful to my wife of forty-eight years for not only being my co-author for some of the contents written, but also for being the one to decipher page after page of my longhand scribbling. I still compose with pen and paper before me since I never learned to type! Sharon is the one of the few who can read my writing and is therefore the one to get the manuscript prepared for editing.

I also want to acknowledge and thank Brenda Hazel, a good friend and Partners in Harvest Pastor, who was one of the first people to read the manuscript in unedited form. As with our first book, *The World's Greatest Revivals,* she helped me think through the content and stay on track with the subject at hand.

I am also profoundly grateful to Ken and Lisa Norberg, also former Partners in Harvest Pastors, for the hours they spent thoughtfully editing each chapter. Their suggestions, and Lisa's editing skills, honed by her years of functioning as one of the editors of a newspaper in Kalamazoo, Michigan, were invaluable.

And last, but not least, I am indebted to Dinae Hoem, a former administrative assistant of mine during my years as International Coordinator for Partners in Harvest, for her final perusal of the manuscript, catching all "typos" and miscellaneous grammatical errors. Dinae also created the document that was given to the publisher. Thank you, Dinae, for this final product, which is now in the hands of the reader!

PREFACE

My wife, Sharon, and I are convinced that thankfulness, the fruit in a heart rightly tuned to God, will express itself in the fruit of the lips, thanksgiving. Thanksgiving is very important to God. In my case, he even allowed me to struggle for years to enter into the salvation experience, so that I would discover the importance of thanksgiving.

The book that you have in your hands has one purpose, and that is to help people discover the wonder and reality of this important exercise. Our prayer is that it will become foundational in everyone's daily experiential walk with the Father, Son and Holy Spirit.

This book is filled with stories of our journey into the practice of thanksgiving, so it should be easy and fun to read.

It also contains some study from both the Old and New Testaments. We hope the study sections will spur you on in your own understanding and journey into thanksgiving. We also hope that these studies will help you "see" with the eyes of your heart, an activity that the Apostle Paul mentions in Ephesians 1:18, why our thanksgiving is so important to the Father.

Our hope, as you read this book, is that it will help you embrace thanksgiving to our wonderful God as on ongoing lifestyle. We are coming to believe that moving the church of Jesus Christ into a lifestyle of thanksgiving is not only important to the growth and development of our own individual walks with God, but that it is a key element in preparing the Bride for the Bridegroom. That is the wonderful event that we in the Body of Christ are walking towards. We read about it in Revelation 19:6–7:

> Then I heard something like the voice of a great multitude and like the sound of many waters, and like the sound of mighty peals of thunder, saying, "Hallelujah! For the Lord, our God, the Almighty, reigns. Let us rejoice and be glad and give the glory to Him, for the marriage feast of the Lamb has come and His Bride has made herself ready."

Read, enjoy, and let this book help get you even get more ready for the marriage feast of the Lamb.

CHAPTER 1

THE JOLLY MONKS

In Autumn 2009, the landscape of my life suddenly became distressingly unfamiliar. My wife and I had served in various ministry roles for forty-eight years, including the last fourteen of those years establishing a global network of churches and ministries passionate about life-changing encounters with the love of Father God. As the founding international coordinator of this network, Partners in Harvest (PIH), I had traveled more than 1.2 million miles to at least thirty-five countries.

But in one official act that Autumn, my intense schedule came to nearly a halt. I passed the baton of my PIH leadership role to my assistant, Dan Slade, a former missionary to Ukraine, and committed myself to assisting him while he became acclimated to the responsibilities that for so long had been mine.

I had been in countless settings all over the world, but now my own life seemed foreign. I wasn't sure how to proceed.

As I tried to find my footing during this unsettling season, one night in my Toronto-area home I had a vivid dream. The dream was profoundly significant to me, and I have come to believe that it also is significant to everyone on earth. That is the reason for writing this book.

Here is what I dreamed.

My wife, Sharon, and I had headed out from Toronto by car and were in the last minutes of reaching our destination, a Catholic retreat center somewhere in Pennsylvania. We had just been through a very hectic season in our lives, so we were heeding the advice of some dear friends to seek rest and refreshing at the retreat center, in a monastery.

We knew very little about the center other than its address and the brief recommendation given by our friends, who had been there themselves. "It is a place of great blessing!" they had said, and they expected we would benefit from a stay there as well.

We had been driving for about five hours, traveling through rolling hills, green fields, and occasional woodlands, when we turned off the highway and onto a gravel road. The road wound through the monastery property, perhaps about 40 acres in all. On this calm, overcast day we passed grain fields and vegetable gardens being tended by monks, small groves of fruit trees, and grazing cows. We would later learn that the monastery farm also had laying hens and pigs, and all was used to produce the monastic community's food.

We reached the parking area by the monastery, a cut-stone building perhaps three or four stories high. Here we were greeted by a monk wearing a long, light-brown, hooded robe, the attire of all the 250 monks who lived here. We would find them to be jolly, short in stature, and plump.

I immediately sensed the presence of God on the grounds and continued sensing him as we entered the monastery. The monk helped carry our luggage as he led us to our room, located on the first floor. He opened the room's heavy door, made of hand-hewn oak planks. Inside were simple furnishings, including two single beds and a small table with a lamp. The walls were made of hand-cut stone. Oak beams supported the ceiling. A window looked out onto what appeared to be a small apple orchard.

As Sharon and I settled in, we became aware of a peaceful stillness, an indication of the presence of God. I sensed God smiling upon this place.

The next morning, to our dismay we were suddenly awakened at about 6:00 AM by a loud shout: "THANK YOU, JESUS!" Soon after, another shout erupted: "THANK YOU, JESUS!"

The shouts continued in rapid succession, erupting every few seconds from various rooms along the hallway and penetrating our thick, wooden door. They continued for some time. It seemed each of the 250 monks was waking up with this expression bursting from his heart. We began wishing that the monks had synchronized their alarm clocks, if they even had such things! Why they were doing this was a mystery to us.

At about 8:00 AM we heard a loud knock on our door. The monk serving as our official host had come to invite us to eat breakfast in the dining hall with the other monks and guests.

The large dining hall, which I guessed was at least 150 feet long, with walls of hand-cut stone, had a cavern-like feel. High windows let in scant natural light, and wrought-iron chandeliers hung from the ceiling, crossed by beams of hand-hewn oak. The hall was filled with long, rectangular, rough-cut tables and plank benches, also made from oak. The wood throughout, similar in color to the monks' light-brown robes, brightened the scene.

The jovial monks greeted each other as they arrived for breakfast. Upon seeing us, they shook our hands and hugged us in a warm welcome to our first meal with them. A couple of the monks invited us to join them at one of the tables.

Benches grated across the floor as everyone got seated, about eight to a table. Then breakfast began to arrive. Fellow monks exuberantly delivered dishes filled with steaming-hot scrambled eggs, sizzling bacon slices, hot toast with melted butter—butter churned in their dairy, we were told proudly by one of the serving monks—and fresh, homemade raspberry jam. The sights and smells were enticing!

Before we began to partake of this sumptuous breakfast set before us, one of the monks stood up, folded his hands and bowed his head. He then began in a loud voice, which echoed throughout the hall, to thank Jesus for the meal and everything involved in providing it. He gave thanks in great detail—for the rain and sunshine needed to grow good crops, for the monks' health that made it possible for them to harvest the crops and tend the animals, for the cows that had eaten the good grass and thus produced the rich cream for making such fine butter, for the other animals that were a source of food, for the buildings that housed the animals, and so forth. Fifteen to twenty minutes later, when the monk finally finished his prayer of thanksgiving, we were invited to eat the now lukewarm and somewhat soggy meal.

During the rest of our four days at the monastery, we ate all our meals with these precious men, and the scene was repeated. Meals were delivered to the table piping hot, but they were eaten nearly stone cold because of the time spent in thanksgiving before partaking.

The monks gave thanks at other times as well. As they walked along the monastery's halls and worshiped in their daily chapel service, we heard them say aloud, "THANK YOU, JESUS!" It seemed they gave thanks whenever the mood struck, and it struck often.

Our curiosity compelled us to ask one of the monks at a later meal during our first full day with them, "Why all this emphasis on thanksgiving?"

The monk looked at us rather oddly and asked, "Haven't you read 1 Thessalonians 5:18?" He seemed to be perplexed about why I, as a former pastor, did not know the simplicity of God's will as expressed in that verse.

The verse says, "In everything give thanks, for this is God's will for you in Christ Jesus."

This order of monks had chosen thanksgiving "in everything" as a life mission. They shouted "THANK YOU, JESUS!" in the morning and raised prayers of thanks throughout the day because they were living out their mission moment by moment.

GOD'S MESSAGE TO ME

I woke up from this very detailed dream sensing that it was from God. I was filled with questions, so I asked the Father the questions I have found best to ask after dreaming something that might be from him: "What was that all about? What are you trying to say to me?"

His answer shook me: "Fred, that is where you started in your walk with me, but you have gotten away from it. You have gotten away from thanking me."

I knew he did not mean that I had forgotten to give thanks before eating meals. I knew he meant that thanksgiving had been a very important part of my lifestyle earlier, but somehow it had waned.

How had I started my walk with God? It didn't take long for the memories to return.

CHAPTER 2

HOW DID I GET STARTED?

My dream and God's gentle rebuke brought back to my mind the struggle I went through to begin a relationship with Jesus. Although I grew up in a Christian home and attended a good Baptist church with my parents every Sunday morning, it was not easy for me to connect with the God I heard about there.

From the time I was six years old, every Sunday morning I had the privilege of hearing the basic gospel message tucked into the sermon one way or another. As a result, I knew that I was a sinner, separated from God, and desperately in need of Jesus as my Savior. About the time I reached the age of eight, I responded to an appeal at the end of a Sunday sermon by going forward to receive salvation. I expected to experience something that would validate my response to God's invitation to give my life to him. But nothing happened experientially in my heart.

Over the next nine years I probably responded to salvation appeals about thirty times. The result each time, however, was the same: nothing happened in my heart to confirm a salvation experience. By the time I was seventeen years old, I gave up trying to receive Jesus Christ as my Savior, and some of the Calvinistic teaching I had heard took root in my life in a negative way.

I THOUGHT I WASN'T CHOSEN

From my light brush with John Calvin's teachings I gleaned that some people were the "elect" or the "chosen". Because of my inability to connect with God, I interpreted what I understood of Calvinism to mean that God chooses some people to be his and leaves out the rest, the "unelect", and I was in that group.

Arriving at that philosophical point, it was easy to lose interest in church. I reasoned that, in my case, the salvation issue was moot. What was the use of trying to get saved if I was one of the unelect?

So for the next few years I lived as an unelect person would. Because I loved my parents and my friends from church, I didn't totally abandon those connections to adopt a completely reprobate lifestyle. But my heart attitude was, "I am out of here!" I began doing things my parents would have been shocked to discover I was doing, such as gambling and viewing pornography.

Thankfully, during that day and age, alcohol and drugs were not readily accessible to youth. Also, I was on the high school track team, and because of the effect smoking could have on the ability to run, my track coach threatened to eliminate anyone from the team who smoked. So I avoided those potential traps.

I did stay involved with Youth for Christ. I enjoyed being with my church friends at YFC meetings, and I enjoyed the meetings themselves, which were full of fun. Those continued activities and friendships helped prevent me from getting into the major trouble that loomed on the path I had chosen.

THE SNOWLESS SNOW CAMP

Fortunately for me, during my first year of college, some of my Christian friends, who were concerned about what was happening in my life, invited me to go to a Christian winter retreat with them in the mountains outside of Los Angeles, near where I grew up. I really enjoyed snow sports and agreed to go for that reason.

I showed up with my toboggan at the cabin where we would stay, happily finding 2½ feet of snow there. To my dismay, however, it began to rain, and within four hours of my arrival, all the snow was gone. We had nothing to do while it rained but stay inside the cabin and listen to the speaker who had been chosen for the weekend. He was a popular disc jockey from one of the local, secular radio stations—who also was a Christian. The youth leaders used him to fill the long rain-filled hours with many speaking sessions.

I was angry and believed that God had ruined my fun on purpose, so I sat in the back of the room during his sessions and sulked. Finally, after about three sessions, I began to listen because I was bored and the speaker was humorous. In one of those sessions he told his life story, and it was nearly identical to mine! He also had prayed many times when he was growing up to receive Jesus as his Savior, but nothing happened experientially to him to confirm his salvation.

At the end of his message he said: "I sense that some of you here can identify personally with me and my story. If you are one of those and would like to chat with me after I close this session, I am available to talk with you personally."

It took me probably less than a second to get to him. He suggested that we go to a back room to chat, and I gladly went with him. After he heard my story, he asked me if I would like to pray the sinner's prayer with him, a prayer that I knew by heart. When I reached the part about inviting Jesus into my life, just like every time before, nothing happened experientially within me.

When I told the disc jockey that, he said: "Well, Fred, you forgot a very important key. You forgot to thank Jesus for coming into your life and saving you." He suggested that we go through the prayer once again, this time adding at the end, "Thank you, Jesus, for coming into my life." I thought to myself, "What do I have to lose?"

So I began again. "Jesus, I'm very sorry for turning my back on you and getting into some bad stuff—sin. Please forgive me, Lord, and come into my life and make me new." I then tacked onto the end, "Thank you for coming into my life."

The disc jockey prompted me to thank Jesus once again, and then again, so I did. After three times of thanking Jesus as instructed, I realized that something was beginning to happen! I was experiencing something I can only describe as a rush of life within me. I spontaneously shouted at the top of my voice, "Thank you, Jesus, for coming into my life!" for the next 45 minutes!

My outburst of joy was loud enough that my friends in another part of the cabin could hear it. Joy hit them as well, because they had been praying for my salvation for a long time. I came out of that back room with a big smile on my face and tears streaming from my eyes. My friends rushed to me and hugged me, warmly welcoming me into the family of God.

We are all so unique and, for whatever the reason, I was one who needed a clear and strong experiential touch of God as a confirmation of my entrance into salvation through Jesus Christ. It is amazing that the God of the universe stoops down to meet us each one in our uniqueness! Some of you were able to lay hold of your salvation without an immediate tangible touch from God. You entered into your salvation by faith alone as you prayed the sinner's prayer!

What a glorious family we are a part of, each with their own story to tell! But we all are thankful for the gift of his salvation, being rescued out of the kingdom of darkness as Paul mentions in Colossians 1:13 and brought into the kingdom of light.

THANKSGIVING, THE KEY TO RELYING ON GOD

That day totally changed my life. I got saved, yes, but I also began to see the key role of thanksgiving in walking with God. Thanksgiving was the catalyst for my salvation experience.

Thanksgiving is the key that opens the door of faith, and *"The just shall live by faith."* (Romans 1:17 NKJV) Thanksgiving is an expression of our dependency on God and positions us to rely on and receive from him.

To cement these realities within me, a few months after my salvation experience God led me to a Bible school in England. The school, operated by Capernwray Missionary Fellowship of Torchbearers, now Torchbearers International, took me into the next level of thanksgiving.

The Bible school was deeply rooted in the truth that walking with Jesus Christ is meant to be a 24-hours-a-day, 7-days-a-week, 52-weeks-a-year experience of seeing what Father God is doing and doing those things with him. This is the way Jesus' walk with his Father is described in John 5:19–20:

> "Truly, truly, I say to you, the Son can do nothing of Himself, unless it is something He sees the Father doing; for whatever the

Father does, these things the Son also does in like manner. For the Father loves the Son, and shows Him all things that He Himself is doing; and the Father will show Him greater works than these, so that you will marvel."

My six months at the Bible school also taught me to live in the expectancy that God would lead me each day into doing works he had already planned for me to accomplish, as stated in Ephesians 2:10: *"For we are His workmanship, created in Christ Jesus for good works, which God prepared beforehand so that we should walk in them."*

God was not burdening me with accomplishing good works on my own. Rather, I could rely on him doing the works through me because he is within me. The Apostle Paul describes this freeing reality in Colossians 1:26–27: *"... the mystery which has been hidden from the past ages and generations, but has now been manifested to His saints ... which is Christ in you, the hope of glory."*

At the Bible school, thankfulness was seen as the simplest expression of dependency on God to be who he is through us. So I learned that the key to walking in good works was to keep a flow of thankfulness ringing in my heart, even when things didn't go quite the way I had expected.

This made my Christian walk exciting. It made each day a new gift from God to be enjoyed with him as I saw what he was doing in me and through me. I was so thankful to him, not only for salvation from sin, but for the fact that he wanted to live life to the fullest each day through me!

To top it all off, he revealed to me my life's partner during this Bible school and gave both of us some direction about the future.

CHAPTER 3

ALWAYS GIVING THANKS

Early in our marriage, God began preparing Sharon and me for a major segment of our journey—living in Sweden for eleven years by faith. I had seen the spiritual needs of youth from that secular country during my time in Europe, and felt called to minister there.

But before we headed overseas, I graduated from Denver Seminary in Colorado, and then Sharon and I were invited to come on staff with a lovely, older Baptist couple in Seaside, central California. I was the assistant pastor serving in the youth and children's ministries, and Sharon helped with the youth ministry and taught a Sunday school class with me for young married couples.

The church was near Fort Ord, a US Army post where soldiers were undergoing advanced infantry training before being sent to Vietnam. Sharon and I were also being equipped by God during our eighteen months in the area before heading to Sweden, and our equipping involved some pain.

CALIFORNIA SHAKING

We came to serve at Seaside unaware of how prideful we were and how confident we were that we would be a big help to any church. Part of this confidence came from our recent history. God had given us favor wherever we had served as youth leaders.

Also, I had just completed an internship at one of the best churches in California, where we had seen the dynamics of a successfully-run church.

To top it all off, I now had my Master of Divinity degree.

Subconsciously, we thought we were God's gift to the Seaside church. After eighteen months with that attitude emanating from us, I was fired. We left town humbled by what seemed like total failure, wondering if we ever would be capable of serving God at all.

It became evident to us that, before going to Seaside, we had begun to trust in ourselves because of our successes in ministry. God used our time of humbling to bring us back to the simplicity of being totally dependent on him. The pain and confusion we felt did not keep us from thanking him for the revelation of the prideful attitude that had formed in us. That revelation pushed us closer to God with new desperation.

READING AS WE WAITED

Carrying a sense of total failure and unsure what to do next, we moved in with my parents in southern California. My father worked in filmmaking for Moody Institute of Science, affiliated with Moody Bible Institute, and helped us find jobs within that company to pay our bills. The jobs we were given were simple and paid only minimum wage. The dream of going to Sweden was still in our hearts, but we had some questions: was God still going to take us there? If so, when would he feel we were ready to go?

In our bedroom in the family home was a bookcase. One evening we went through the bookshelves and picked out two books to read together—the biography of George Mueller, who led a large orphanage work in Bristol, England, and the biography of Hudson Taylor, a pioneer missionary to inland China.

As we read these books out loud to each other in the evenings, we were awed by the lifestyles of these two men. Their trust in God was simple, yet amazing. They lived in the miraculous on a daily basis.

GEORGE MUELLER

We read that a young George Mueller in the 1800s began to be impacted by seeing vast numbers of children living on the streets of Bristol in total squalor. Most of them were only six to twelve years old. Many had helped their families survive by working in wool and cotton factories, doing jobs no one else would do, such as picking up tufts of wool and cotton that had accumulated on the factory floors under weaving machines. Some of these children suffered such severe lung infections from exposure to wool and cotton dust that they could no longer work, so they were tossed out to live on the streets. Many of these street urchins, as they were called, turned to thievery. Many of them died young.

The Lord spoke to Mueller about opening a house for some of the street urchins. By faith he acquired his first home, where thirty of these children could be housed and nursed back to health. As the years passed, God continually led Mueller to take in larger and larger numbers of children. By the end of his ministry, he was responsible for more than three thousand orphans each day.

How did he manage that financially? By faith! He was not a wealthy man, and few churches at that time had a vision to help street children. He did not send out appeal letters, or travel around raising funds. His simple *modus operandi* was to "move men through God by prayer alone." He would thank God daily in his prayers, knowing that God loved the children and would provide for them.

He faced times when he went to bed knowing that there were no provisions for meals the next day. God heard every one of his prayers, as proven in this prayer recorded in the book: "God, there is nothing in the kitchen for tomorrow; but you know that the kids are used to eating porridge with milk each morning. They are also used to having a slice of bread with breakfast. Thank you for what you are going to do." After praying that prayer, he fell asleep.

The next morning, as they all sat down at empty breakfast tables, Mueller and the children prayed a simple prayer of thanksgiving together. Suddenly the back door to the eating area opened with a bang. In walked three men who had not been able to sleep that night—a baker who had been up all night baking bread; a dairy farmer who had been prompted to deliver fresh, warm milk to the orphanage before doing his normal chores for that day; and a farmer who had loaded his wagon with oats to bring to the orphanage. Breakfast was served as soon as the oats were cooked.

This was only one incident among many when God demonstrated his faithfulness to Mueller and the children under his care. Soon God was entrusting many funds into Mueller's hands, some of which he funneled into the hands of Hudson Taylor, who was pioneering missionary work in inland China.

HUDSON TAYLOR

Like Mueller, Hudson Taylor also subscribed to the premise that he would move men only through God by prayer alone. He prayed in finances for not only himself and his family, but also for other missionaries who served with him.

These first missionaries to inland China didn't find dwellings to live in that were anything like those back home in England. The available foods were new and confusing to them. Disease was rampant and fevers easily caught. They had to learn a new language with many dialects. However, because of their fervor and persistence, eventually the China Inland Mission became the largest and most successful mission organization of that era.

Taylor's trust in the Lord, and thanksgiving to him, prevailed through the deaths of two wives and several of his children from the harshness of the conditions where they were called to minister. He didn't let his circumstances overcome him. He kept His eyes turned to the goodness of God.

This is the first line of a hymn he often sang when he received bad news: "*Jesus, I am resting, resting in the joy of what thou art; I am finding out the greatness of thy loving heart.*"

INSPIRED TO GO OVERSEAS BY FAITH

God used the biographies of these two godly heroes powerfully in our lives. The result was we felt prompted to go to Sweden by faith. If God could provide for George Mueller in England and Hudson Taylor in China, he could provide for Fred and Sharon Wright in Sweden.

Our mission leader, Major W. Ian Thomas of Capernwray Missionary Fellowship of Torchbearers, confirmed this to us in his acceptance letter that welcomed us to work within his organization: "If God wants you there in Sweden, he will provide what you need. If he doesn't, he won't."

In some strange way, that comforted us. We left for Europe on April 1, 1970. We had not sent out appeal letters for financial help, but we had sent out prayer letters informing our friends and family members about our move. We wanted prayer backing for going to secular Sweden.

Just before it was time to purchase our one-way plane tickets to Europe, our first unsolicited surprise gift came from a young couple in the church we were attending. We also received the promise of $25 a month from some college friends. Each time God provided some money through someone, we were amazed and delighted by his provision and said a big "THANK YOU, JESUS!"

PROVISION FOR FIRST STEPS

When we boarded the plane that April 1, our initial destination was England, where our mission's headquarters was located. We arrived in time to attend the mission's spring Bible school. We wanted to renew acquaintances with the leaders there and be immersed in Bible study before setting foot in Sweden. This also meant that we had a roof over our heads and three meals a day for April and May.

We had been invited to live with Christian and Martha Bastke in Kristiansand, Norway, for the month of June. The Bastkes were the Scandinavian representatives of our mission organization. They not only provided a roof over our heads, but also helped us become familiar with the Scandinavian lifestyle.

Years before, in 1962, Christian had been one of the teachers during the mission's winter Bible school that we had attended. He had been kind enough to invite me to travel with him after the school ended. I helped him as he ran a youth vacation event in Berlin that included sightseeing and Bible sessions, and then we traveled to Denmark, Norway and Sweden, where he led conferences and Bible studies for young adults. It was as I saw Christian in action and the needs of the Scandinavian youth that God began drawing me toward ministry in Scandinavia. In other words, God started preparing me in 1962 for our ministry in Scandinavia eight years later.

In 1971, Christian would launch a spring Bible school on an island near Kristiansand and invite Sharon and me to help him run it. The school, on Flekkerøy, would continue for three springs and be a wonderful part of our training for what God had called us to do in Sweden.

We were so thankful for God's provision, not only for housing and food, but for fellowship with and training from experienced leaders. "THANK YOU, JESUS!"

Our first major faith issue was housing.

NEEDING A ROOF OVER OUR HEADS

We arrived in Jönköping, Sweden, in July 1970, just in time to help disciple some of the many thousands of young people who were becoming believers through the Jesus People movement of the 1970s. We quickly found that the cost of living in Sweden was at least double that in North America, so we wondered whether we would be able to afford food after paying for a place to live.

Just finding affordable housing required a miracle. Sharon and I had come to a cold, wet, dark, and sometimes unfriendly country with no permanent place to stay. We had housing for our first three months through a contact of our mission leader. The contact, Karl Frandell, was a leader in a denomination that had an apartment in Jönköping for missionaries needing a time of rest. It just happened to be empty from July through September, and was graciously offered to us to use during that vacancy.

The apartment was on the second floor of a former railroad station—situated on the main line for trains traveling from the east coast to the west coast of south-central Sweden. About thirty-five trains a day roared past our home. The concussion caused by their speed when they passed was unnerving at first. But our bodies and minds adjusted so that eventually we didn't even notice when a train went by. Our occasional guests, however, were startled when a train shook our shelter. Often we were asked how we slept there, or if we slept at all. But our response was, "THANK YOU, JESUS!"

The weeks passed, and soon we were crying out for our next living quarters, careful to thank God for his promise to supply our needs. At the very last moment, a couple from a Baptist church we were attending offered us the use of their summer home, near Jönköping, for a very nominal fee. But it was available for just the six winter months before their family arrived for the summer.

The home was a primitive farmhouse, not winterized. It had a two-burner electric hot plate for cooking and one cold-water faucet in the kitchen. We couldn't heat the house adequately, so we often sat in our sleeping bags to keep warm. We had to keep the water trickling from the faucet so it wouldn't freeze. The house had a toilet room but no bathtub, so taking baths required heating water on the hot plate, one kettle at a time. You should have seen me in the blue, plastic tub we bought for bathing! I looked like a turtle on its back, because only my rear end fit in the tub and my arms and legs dangled over the sides.

But we were so thankful for a roof over our heads during the winter! God had supplied our need. "THANK YOU, JESUS!" As summer approached, we began to thank God in advance for our next place to live. Remember, there was no Craigslist, Google or eBay then, so with our still-limited Swedish, we had to read newspaper ads to see if there was any available housing that we could afford. With only days to spare, we found an ad for an upstairs apartment in a family home even farther away from Jönköping than the farmhouse.

When we went to the door to be interviewed by the elderly woman who lived on the ground floor, her son also was there, apparently to appraise us. Somehow, despite our limited Swedish, they felt we would be a safe couple to have living there.

Once again the Lord had supplied us with housing, but this time for an unlimited period! Although the extra miles from town would mean increased costs to attend our Swedish classes, we were so grateful to be allowed to rent this place, which was quiet and warm, and had a bathtub, a stove, and even hot water! Our expectant thanksgiving turned into jubilant thanksgiving: "THANK YOU, JESUS! THANK YOU, THANK YOU, JESUS!"

The son owned a furniture store and gave us a good price on a sofa that made into a bed, as well as on a bookcase and a coffee table. These furnished our front room, but the rest of our apartment was empty except for the kitchen, where we had an old table and chair set that the owners had left in place

ENCOURAGED BY GOD'S SUPPLY

Those were highlights of our first three years in Sweden. We had few ministry opportunities then, and the ones we had were in Norway, Germany, and England, where I taught in Capernwray Bible schools. There was very little to report in our prayer letters to our friends other than that we were studying Swedish. The only evidence for us that God wanted us in Sweden was that he supplied our needs, a major source of encouragement, and we kept on thanking him.

The lessons we had learned were about to be taken to the next level. Those who are faithful with little will be entrusted by God with even more, says Matthew 25:21. We had been faithful with giving thanks, and growing in thanksgiving means receiving bigger challenges and bigger opportunities to see God provide and demonstrate his faithfulness and love.

CHAPTER 4

PRACTISING THANKSGIVING

During our first three years in Sweden we had the opportunity to see how the European Capernwray Bible schools and conference centers operated. Each of those years I taught for two to three-week periods at all five centers—in England, Germany, Austria and Spain.

We also took groups of Swedish young people to the centers for what we called house parties, two-week vacation events in the summer that included sightseeing, lots of sports and games, and morning and evening Bible sessions. The vacations were evangelistic in purpose, and although many of the participants had been drawn only by the chance to experience another country and culture, many of them met the Lord Jesus at these events.

A NEW STEP IN FAITH

We decided to host a vacation event in Sweden, so we rented a conference facility for it near our home. We secured some catering help and organized trips to the nearby famous crystal factories and to Sweden's capital, Stockholm. We advertised and then waited for young people to register. This was our first time to require funds for something bigger than our own needs as a couple. We were excited about this new step and thanked God for what he was going to do.

He more than answered our prayers! About 150 guests came that summer in 1972. Everyone seemed to have a good time, and many became believers in the Lord. At the end of the two weeks we were tired but jubilant—so jubilant that we began to dream about having a facility of our own in Sweden. We thought perhaps a small farm, with just enough acreage to support ourselves and the guest students, would be perfect.

YET A BIGGER STEP IN FAITH

We had no funds for such a venture, but we were filled with faith that God was ready to take us to the next level of ministry. So we began praying that fall for what we thought we wanted— a small farm. Within two weeks, a Swedish friend told us that he knew someone who wanted to sell an old health spa, located about an hour and a half by car southeast of Jönköping, to a Christian group. This property had seventeen acres, mostly forested, and twenty-five old buildings, some more than 200 years old and in different degrees of usability. Two buildings were winterized and ready to use. They came with furniture, linens, cutlery, pots and pans, dishes—the works. All we would have to do, besides get the funds to purchase the site, was move in.

The property was bigger than we had envisioned, but we presented the possibility of acquiring it to Major Thomas the following week, as he just happened to be holding meetings in our part of Sweden. When he heard about the opportunity and was taken to see the property, he grew quite excited, although he knew there were no funds available for such an investment.

Major Thomas was in Texas the next week for an annual meeting of the US Capernwray board, and mentioned the property to those at the meeting. Afterward a man there offered to buy the site for our use, even though he had not seen it. He felt he could trust Major Thomas' evaluation of the property, and his only stipulation was that we keep it in good shape.

Suddenly we had land and buildings to use and maintain.

SCHOOL IN SWEDEN
BECOMES A REALITY

Just one year after hosting the vacation event at a rented facility, we welcomed our first forty-five students to Holsby Brunn Bible School and Conference Center on the newly acquired property in south-central Sweden. The students hadn't paid their fees yet, so our prayers became focused on how to feed them and our newly-arrived staff members without having cash on hand.

Our need for staff members had been wonderfully met. A lovely, older couple from the United States, who had been missionaries in Africa, asked if they could come and help us. John "Pop" Nickle had experience in construction and became our maintenance man and renovator. His wife, Eleanor, who soon became "Mom" to everyone, coordinated the kitchen. A former student of ours, Katrin Bjuhr, who had attended one of the Norwegian Bible schools we had helped lead during our first three years in Scandinavia, became our secretary. She was a Swede who had grown up in Stockholm, so she helped us move more smoothly in the realm of Swedish governmental requirements. Major Thomas sent us a couple who had been pastors in the States, Wally and Donna Schoon, to act as associates and teachers.

Sharon and I were amazed at how quickly God had orchestrated everything, and our prayer letters got a lot more exciting! We were so thankful to the Lord for not only providing a venue for our use, but also a hardworking staff and, of course, our forty-five students.

GROWING PAINS

Enrollment increased the next three years, and the students were rapidly outgrowing the school's lecture hall, a big lounge in the main building. God drew our attention to an old summer chapel on the property that could seat 150 people on its old-style wooden pews. We had used it for our summer program, but now began to look at it through different lenses.

Those lenses cast light on the enormity of turning the uninsulated chapel into a winterized building. The cost was only one of several concerns. We tried to set some money aside from the student fees each year for such needs, but this renovation project would require much more than insulation, wallboard, and paint. We also wanted to create a second-floor lounge for the students to use outside of classes. Just the thought of getting the needed permits made our minds spin.

But since God had given us the idea, we turned to him in prayer and began thanking him for what he was going to do. We realized how dependent we were on him to complete this project. It was interesting to see how he began to make things work.

First, a friend from our days in Jönköping heard about our plans to renovate the chapel and volunteered to oversee the project. A building engineer, he assured us that our plans, including the second-floor lounge, were feasible. He began to get the required permits, arrange for architectural plans, and estimate the amount of materials needed.

Second, for the first year of the project, God sent us a group of Mennonite students from Canada. Many of them had built barns and displayed godly work ethics by working hard. Our school curriculum included a work day each week, and the male students that year rose to the challenge, even volunteering to work extra afternoons.

Much of the initial labor involved removing dry rot that had accumulated over decades in the chapel. A "mole patrol" was formed that dug around the original floor joists and hauled out by hand buckets of debris.

When it came time to create the second-story floor, the Mennonite barn builders found a way to raise the needed beams in place without using an expensive crane. Someone with welding and blacksmithing experience was on the scene just as those skills were needed.

We continued to be amazed at how God orchestrated all these details. Our thanksgiving increased throughout the project as we saw God supplying things we didn't even know we would require.

Because of that renovation project and others, the school grew from a capacity of forty-five students per term to a student body of ninety-eight the last year we were there. But renovating the chapel and other buildings to accommodate the growing number of students was not our only challenge during our eight years at Holsby Brunn.

WHAT DO YOU MEAN
WE HAVE NO ELECTRICITY?!

Several times we faced electrical outages that lasted for days after storms toppled trees onto our power lines. Much creativity was required to cook meals for from fifty to one hundred people without using electricity. We had to improvise meals that could be cooked over a campfire in one humongous cooking pot.

Our toilets wouldn't flush without electricity, so we also had to organize a crew to keep 50-gallon oil drums, placed in each general toilet room, full of water from our well. That made water available for scooping out and pouring into the tanks.

Our heating system also required electricity for pumping water to each radiator in the main buildings, so those buildings became quite cold after several days, prompting the girls in the girls' dormitory to share beds at night and double up on blankets.

WHAT DO YOU MEAN
THE BARN IS ON FIRE?!

Power outages weren't the only ordeal. One night our big barn—where we stored building supplies, tools and firewood—caught fire after a student left rags that had been used to rub linseed oil into refinished furniture near a stack of wood trim. The results of the spontaneous combustion were dramatic.

Students ran buckets of water to the inferno until volunteer firefighters arrived. Despite all the efforts, the building was consumed before our eyes.

We had lost not only the contents, which also included a woodworking shop, other shops, and a car, but now we had no place to store supplies for our renovation projects. These losses prompted us to modify some of our renovation goals. Yet we thanked the Lord for his protection during what could have been a bigger tragedy.

THANKSGIVING, FAITH GROW

God used these hard times to build camaraderie among the students and staff members. How thankful we were that God could turn around negative situations and bring such good from them.

We also continued growing in faith, from having faith just for our own needs to having faith for all the unexpected situations that arose as we lived in community. In each instance God was faithful, many times supplying our needs even before we knew we had them. As our faithful God showed his hand upon us for the good, time after time, how could we not be thankful?

For the many times he walked ahead of us, preparing the way; for having people in place to help us get done what needed to be done; for his protection of staff members and students during all the construction projects; for being with us during those hard times for which we were unprepared, THANK YOU, JESUS!

CHAPTER 5

JESUS THANKS HIS FATHER

As I reread stories about Jesus in the Gospels, I found that thanksgiving played a vital role in how he related to Father God and conducted his ministry.

Many people ascribe the miracles that Jesus performed to his being the Son of God with all the power and authority that inherently belong to each member of the Godhead. But Paul, in Philippians 2:5–7, reminds us of Jesus' state while he was on earth:

> Have this attitude in yourselves which was also in Christ Jesus, who, although He existed in the form of God, did not regard equality with God a thing to be grasped, but emptied Himself, taking the form of a bond-servant, and being made in the likeness of men.

Why did Jesus come to earth "emptied?" He came to model for us how we were meant to live—dependent on God. Let's look at how Jesus described his dependency on the Father [God] here on earth, as recorded in John 5:19–20:

> "Truly, truly, I say to you, the Son can do nothing of Himself, unless it is something He sees the Father doing; for whatever the Father does, these things the Son also does in like manner. For the Father loves the Son, and shows Him all things that He Himself is doing."

Jesus watched to see what the Father was doing, and joined him in doing those things each day. His utter dependency on the Father led to the many adventures they shared while Jesus was here.

This is a picture of the relationship we can have as well with God as Father. Many times in the New Testament, Jesus calls God "your Father" and "your heavenly Father".

Jesus also demonstrated his dependency on his Father through thanksgiving. Here are some examples.

THE FEEDING OF THE FIVE THOUSAND

The Gospel of Matthew recounts how Jesus fed five thousand men, as well as the women and children accompanying them, though the available resources were few. The people had gathered around Jesus and lingered until evening, when they became hungry. Jesus' disciples told him that the only food they had found among the crowd was five loaves of bread and two fish. In Matthew 14:19–20, we read what Jesus did next:

> Ordering the people to sit down on the grass, He took the five loaves and the two fish, and looking up toward heaven, He blessed the food, and breaking the loaves He gave them to the disciples, and the disciples gave them to the crowds, and they all ate and were satisfied. They picked up what was left over of the broken pieces, twelve full baskets.

The word "blessed" that's used here comes from the Greek word *eulogeo,* which means to praise, to celebrate with praises, or to acknowledge God's goodness with a desire for his glory.

THE FEEDING OF THE FOUR THOUSAND

Another miracle, the feeding of four thousand people, happened similarly, as recorded in Matthew 15:32–37 and Mark 8:6–8. This time the disciples had seven loaves and a few fish to disperse under Jesus' direction. Here is Mark's account:

> And He directed the people to sit down on the ground; and taking the seven loaves, He gave thanks and broke them, and started giving them to His disciples to serve to them, and they served them to the people. They also had a few small fish; and after He had blessed them, He ordered these to be served as well. And they ate and were satisfied; and they picked up seven large baskets full of what was left over of the broken pieces.

Jesus demonstrated His dependence on the Father by giving thanks for what he had and for what he knew the Father was going to supply. Then, as he broke the few pieces of bread and fish, they multiplied.

In other words, thanksgiving released the power of God.

Like the disciples, we might say in our situations, "What is this small amount among so many people?" But Jesus thanked the Father for even the little he had, and as he did, a miracle occurred—little became much.

George Mueller and Hudson Taylor experienced this dynamic over and over again. Today's Heidi Baker, ministering to the destitute in Mozambique, experiences it as well. In her book *There is Always Enough,* Heidi recounts not only the multiplication of food for the starving in Mozambique, but also the multiplication of toys for the poor children she loves.

You and I, knowing God the Father as his beloved children,

also can live with a heart attitude of thanksgiving and have our own experiences of the power of God that thankfulness releases.

A LEPER WHO WAS THANKFUL

Thankfulness was key in another interesting incident in the ministry of Jesus, when he encountered ten lepers on the road to Jerusalem, as told in Luke 17:11–19. Verse 13 says the lepers were crying out, *"Jesus, Master, have mercy on us!"* Instead of immediately healing them, Jesus told them to show themselves to the priests, who, under Jewish law, could examine them and, if warranted, declare them free of leprosy. Verse 14 says, *"As they were going, they were cleansed."*

The Greek word for "cleansed" means to make clean, to cleanse from physical stains and dirt or from disease, like leprosy. So the manifestations of leprosy on their bodies were removed.

The account continues in verses 15–16:

> Now one of them, when he saw that he had been healed, turned back, glorifying God with a loud voice, and he fell on his face at His feet, giving thanks to Him. And he was a Samaritan.

The Greek word for "healed" signifies physical healing and also is used figuratively for spiritual healing. (That dual meaning is also found in James 5:16, *"Confess your sins to one another, and pray for one another so that you may be healed."*)

Then Jesus says in verses 17–19:

> "Were there not ten cleansed? But the nine—where are they? Was no one found who returned to give glory to God, except this

foreigner?" And He said to him, "Stand up and go; your faith has made you well."

I believe that Jesus indicates here that the response of thanksgiving is extremely important to the heart of the Father. I also believe that thankfulness preserves a person's healing.

In this same passage, Jesus equates the expression of thankfulness with faith. Thanksgiving is truly a form of faith, because it acknowledges our dependence on the Father.

LAZARUS IS RAISED FROM THE DEAD

Thanksgiving occurs again in Jesus' ministry at Lazarus' tomb. Lazarus had been dead for four days when Jesus arrived at his burial site in Bethany. Yet Jesus stood before the tomb and ordered the stone over its entrance to be removed. What happened next is recorded in John 11:41–43:

> So they removed the stone. Then Jesus raised His eyes, and said, "Father, I thank you that You have heard Me. I know that You always hear Me; but because of the people standing around I said it, so that they may believe that You sent Me." When He had said these things, He cried out with a loud voice, "Lazarus, come forth."

Jesus' expression of thanks demonstrated once again his dependency on the Father and his confidence in what the Father would do. The impossible followed as Lazarus, who had been dead for four days, emerged from the tomb alive.

This tells me that thankfulness draws miracles from the heart of the Father like nothing else.

JESUS' LAST MEAL WITH HIS DISCIPLES

Jesus again expressed his thankfulness in the hours before his crucifixion, his severest trial while on earth. The scene is recorded in Luke 22:17–19, when Jesus observes his last Passover meal with his disciples:

> And when He had taken a cup and given thanks, He said, "Take this and share it among yourselves..." And when He had taken some bread and given thanks, He broke it and gave it to them, saying, "This is My body which is given for you."

I believe that Jesus was not only thanking God for the bread and wine in his customary way, but that he was thanking the Father for what his death would accomplish for us. Thanksgiving prepared Jesus for the agony he was about to suffer.

Throughout his whole life on earth, Jesus only did what he saw the Father doing. Said another way, everything Jesus did, he did in fellowship with God, his Father. The only thing Jesus had to do alone was choose to die. He paves the way with thanksgiving. He knew the importance of thanking the Father in dire situations.

Thanksgiving for Jesus was a way of life, a way that encompassed not only his absolute dependence on the Father for the miraculous, but his means of empowerment to fulfill his destiny—death on the cross to provide salvation for all.

If Jesus thanked the Father as an expression of his utter dependence on the Father, how much more should we express our dependence on the Father as his sons and daughters.

CHAPTER 6

OLD COVENANT THANKFULNESS

When I think of praise and thanksgiving in the Old Testament, I immediately think of the book of Psalms. Many of the songs and poems it contains were written by David, a shepherd boy and musician who became the king of Israel. Based on his writings, he used his long hours alone with his father's sheep profitably, getting to know his God very well.

Here's a brief look at David's expressions of thanks in Psalms before we explore significant shades of meaning in the Hebrew language for the word "thanksgiving."

KING DAVID AND THANKFULNESS

David, and later his son Solomon, reigned during one of Israel's most influential and blessed periods. David was chosen as king by God, who said of him, "*I have found David the son of Jesse, a man after My heart, who will do all My will.*" (Acts 13:22)

Many of the psalms written by this man after God's heart, a worshiper, contain thanksgiving and praise. I will cite only a few examples here:

He delivers me from my enemies;
Surely You lift me above those who rise up against me;
You rescue me from the violent man.

Therefore I will give thanks to You among the nations, O Lord,
And I will sing praises to Your name. (Psalm 18:48–49)

Sing praise to the Lord, you His godly ones,
And give thanks to His holy name. (Psalm 30:4)

You have turned for me my mourning into dancing;
You have loosed my sackcloth and girded me with gladness,
That my soul may sing praise to You and not be silent.
O Lord my God, I will give thanks to You forever. (Psalm 30:11–12)

It is good to give thanks to the Lord
And to sing praises to Your name, O Most High;
To declare Your lovingkindness in the morning
And Your faithfulness by night. (Psalm 92:1–2)

Enter His gates with thanksgiving
And His courts with praise.
Give thanks to Him, bless His Name. (Psalm 100:4)

I gained some insight into verses expressing thanks when, two years ago, I was talking with Sten and Else Thomsen, friends from Denmark, about my dream and how God had used it to release thanksgiving afresh in me. Sten, like David, is a worship leader. He has studied praise, worship and thanksgiving persistently, desiring to lead worship in his church and elsewhere more effectively. He told me something about the two words used for "thanksgiving" in Hebrew that I found very interesting.

The English words "thanksgiving" and "thank" in the Old Testament have been translated from either of two Hebrew words, *yadah* or *todah*, which convey different things.

YADAH

Yadah has a root that means "the extended hand, to throw out the hand, therefore to worship with extended hand." (The opposite meaning is "to bemoan, the wringing of the hands," something many of us do well!)

Psalm 136:1–4 uses *yadah*:

Give thanks to the Lord, for He is good,
For His lovingkindness is everlasting.
Give thanks to the God of gods,
For His lovingkindness is everlasting.
Give thanks to the Lord of lords,
For His lovingkindness is everlasting.
To Him who alone does great wonders,
For His lovingkindness is everlasting.

The rest of the psalm repeats *"His lovingkindness is everlasting"* after each detail recorded of his "great wonders," first the creation, and then the rescue of the Israelites out of Egypt.

Yadah was used in the context of remembering things God had already done, things that God did not want his people to forget or stop thanking him for.

TODAH

Todah comes from the same principle root word as *yadah*, but it is used more specifically. *Todah* literally means "an extension of the hand in adoration, or acceptance." It is used not only for thanking God for things he has already done, but for "things not yet received," for thanking God by faith.

Psalm 100:4–5 is a good example of this use of *todah*. The Jewish people were commanded to give thanks for what God had already done for them, but while also looking forward to future interventions by God on their behalf.

Enter His gates with thanksgiving
And His courts with praise.
Give thanks to Him; bless His name.
For the Lord is good;
His lovingkindness is everlasting
And his faithfulness to all generations.

Let's take a look at three men in the Old Testament who thanked God using *todah*.

KING HEZEKIAH

In 2 Chronicles 29 we read about Hezekiah, who became the king of Judah when he was 25 years old, succeeding the evil ruler Ahaz. 2 Chronicles 28 explains:

But he (*Ahaz*) walked in the ways of the kings of Israel; he also made molten images for the Baals. Moreover, he burned incense in the valley of Ben-hinnom and burned his sons in fire, according to the abominations of the nations whom the Lord had driven out before the sons of Israel. He sacrificed and burned incense on the high places, on the hills and under every green tree. (vv. 2–4)

Conditions under Ahaz's leadership continued to worsen. But fortunately for the kingdom of Judah, his son, Hezekiah, had a heart like David's and did what was right. One of the first things Hezekiah did was open and repair the doors of God's house, the temple. Then he gathered the priests and the Levites there and gave them this injunction, recounted in 2 Chronicles 29:5–7:

> "Listen to me, O Levites. Consecrate yourselves now, and consecrate the house of the Lord, the God of your fathers, and carry the uncleanness out from the holy place. For our fathers have been unfaithful and have done evil in the sight of the Lord our God, and have forsaken Him and turned their faces away from the dwelling place of the Lord, and have turned their backs. They have also shut the doors of the porch and put out the lamps, and have not burned incense or offered burnt offerings in the holy place to the God of Israel."

It was in Hezekiah's heart to reinstitute worship and praise to the Lord in the temple. So the priests began to cleanse the temple before reconsecrating it to the Lord.

Once the temple was cleansed, Hezekiah led an assembly there in making sacrifices to the Lord. The Levites, with musical instruments from the time of David, and the priests, with their trumpets, played music to the Lord until all the burnt offerings had been presented.

Then King Hezekiah said, as recorded in verse 31:

> "Now that you have consecrated yourselves to the Lord, come near and bring sacrifices and thank offerings to the house of the Lord." And the assembly brought sacrifices and thank offerings, and all those who were willing brought burnt offerings."

The word used for "thank" here is *todah*. Hezekiah and the people thanked God for the restoration of worship in the temple and also for what that would mean to them in the future, including protection and guidance as they obeyed and worshiped the Lord.

THE PROPHET NEHEMIAH

Nehemiah was serving King Artaxerxes, the ruler of Persia, as a cupbearer when he learned that his fellow Jews, who had survived captivity in a foreign land and returned to Jerusalem, were living there in great distress. The city wall had been broken down and its gates burned.

Nehemiah mourned, fasted and prayed to the Lord, confessing the sins of Israel. He reminded God that God had said of Israel:

"If you return to Me and keep My commandments and do them, though those of you who have been scattered were in the most remote part of the heavens, I will gather them from there and will bring them to the place where I have chosen to cause My name to dwell." (Nehemiah 1:9)

Then Nehemiah was released by Artaxerxes to return to Jerusalem to help rebuild the wall. When it was finished, the wall was dedicated, as recorded in Nehemiah 12:27–30:

Now at the dedication of the wall of Jerusalem they sought out the Levites from all their places, to bring them to Jerusalem so that they might celebrate the dedication with gladness, with hymns of thanksgiving (todah) and with songs to the accompaniment of cymbals, harps and lyres. So the sons of the singers were assembled

from the district around Jerusalem, and from the villages of the
Netophathites, from Beth-gilgal and from their fields in Geba and
Azmaveth, for the singers had built themselves villages around
Jerusalem. So the priests and Levites purified themselves; they also
purified the people, the gates and the wall.

The thanksgiving, or *todah*, was for what had been accomplished and also for what that would mean to Israel in the future.

THE PROPHET JONAH

The book of Jonah is an interesting account of a prophet who
was given a mission by God that he tried to avoid. Instead of
simply obeying God and going inland to Nineveh to cry out
against its sinfulness, he boarded a ship in Joppa, on the shores
of the Mediterranean Sea, and headed toward Tarshish.

Not long into the voyage, God caused a storm to develop
that threatened to break up the ship. The crew surmised that
some deity was unhappy with someone on board, and cast
lots to see who the culprit was. The lots fell on Jonah, who
explained his avoided commission from God and offered to
be thrown into the sea. Once the men threw him overboard,
to their amazement the storm immediately stopped.

God caused a "great fish" to swallow Jonah, so Jonah found
himself in its stomach—for three days and three nights. Imagine
swirling around hour after hour in vile digestive juices along
with whatever else the fish had swallowed! This prompted a
fervent prayer by Jonah that is recorded in Jonah 2:1–9. The
verse I want to highlight is verse 9:

"But I will sacrifice to You with the voice of thanksgiving (*todah*).
That which I have vowed I will pay. Salvation is from the Lord."

Jonah made a sacrifice of thanksgiving to the Lord before he knew whether the Lord would save him. It was a sacrifice of praise offered before any evidence of any type of salvation. It was an exercise in faith before his rescue.

After Jonah gave his sacrifice of thanksgiving, God commanded the fish to vomit him up onto land. A now-submissive Jonah hurried to Nineveh to do at last what the Lord had asked him to do.

THANKFULNESS AND OUR PERSPECTIVE OF GOD

We also are called upon to give thanks before receiving God's help. Hebrews 13:15 says, *"Through Him then, let us continually offer up a sacrifice of praise to God, that is, the fruit of lips that give thanks to His name."*

Knowing that God is good, that he operates out of faithfulness and lovingkindness, we do not thank him only for what we already have received but for what he is about to do in our lives.

When we are thanking and praising God—whether as a sacrifice, or from an overflow in our hearts after having just seen his salvation in some area of our lives, or when remembering his past great wonders—he becomes bigger in our perspective.

Psalm 69:30 expresses it this way:

I will praise the name of God with song
And magnify Him with thanksgiving.

Psalm 40:16 says:

Let all who seek You rejoice and be glad in You;
Let those who love Your salvation say continually,
"The Lord be magnified."

Our thanksgiving helps us align our perspective of God with who he is.

GIVING THANKS FOR
THE UNREALIZED IN SWEDEN

When we were leading the Bible school in Sweden, initially most of the students there were from English-speaking countries. Very few were from Scandinavia, which was the target land in our hearts.

We were pondering how to change this when a guest speaker came from Wycliffe Bible Translators. She asked us why the Lord would put us in Sweden if we were not drawing our students from Scandinavia. At that time, only two of our sixty-five students were Scandinavians. The guest speaker's question challenged us to begin praying specifically that more Scandinavians would attend the school.

Our prayers began to be full of *todah* thanksgiving, so we prayed more like this: "Thank (*yadah*) you, Father, for providing a wonderful facility for the school and for our needs. We know that we are here to also train and disciple Scandinavian youth. Lord, we have only two Scandinavian students right now, but we thank (*todah*) you that you will bring in many more. We are asking you for eight next year and we thank you in advance for bringing them."

The next year he brought ten Scandinavian students to the school. We then felt bold enough to pray for twelve for the next year, and fifteen came. So we then prayed and thanked him by faith for eighteen for the next year, and twenty came.

During the last year that Sharon and I were at Holsby Brunn Bible School and Conference Center, twenty-eight of the ninety-eight students were Scandinavians. Many of them became leaders of churches and ministries in Scandinavia.

We are not trying to turn thanksgiving into a magic formula, or a way of manipulating God to do what is in our hearts. Instead, we have found that thanking God before the answers come helps build our faith. Many times we believers have a begging approach to prayer, which can hinder faith and, therefore, hinder results. Seeing the release that thanksgiving brings dramatically changed how we prayed.

CHAPTER 7

THANKSGIVING, THE KEY TO HEALING

I had just given a message during the Sunday morning service in a church in Marysville, Washington when a nurse approached me with some interesting information. I had shared what God had been revealing to me about thanksgiving since my dream about the jolly monks in Pennsylvania. This nurse knew of a medical study that had been done in recent years that showed that thanksgiving has a profound effect on speeding up the healing process in hospital patients.

Medical personnel in hospitals involved in this study would take notice when patients were not responding to medication, or when broken bones were not mending as they should. In those cases, an amazing experimental therapy then was implemented. The nurses would give those patients journals and ask them to write down daily everything that came to their minds that they were thankful for.

The patients who did the thanksgiving exercise in earnest soon found that the healing process in their bodies began to speed up. The nurse said the study found that medications being taken worked better, bones mended more quickly, and atrophied muscles were strengthened faster in those patients.

MY HEALING PROCESS AFTER MY STROKE

I credit my own recovery from a stroke in December of 2009 to God's response to the prayers raised up around the world for me and the thankfulness that God released in me. Stroke is not uncommon in my family line. Mine, caused by a massive bleed on the right side of my brain, left me unable to negotiate even the short distance to the toilet without help from two nurses. I also couldn't think or talk coherently.

The stories that my family tells about my first week in St. Michael's Hospital in Toronto still bring chuckles to us all. My thoughts were so garbled that I mistakenly assumed I was in my home, thus I couldn't correctly interpret things going on around me. Evidently I was amazed that the "little girls in green" were so nice to come to our house to help us and to bring the hospital equipment as well! I was also afraid that our neighbors weren't going to like the parking meters that had been installed on the street in front of our homes. That concern must have come from hearing my visitors commenting on how expensive it was to park in downtown Toronto.

Within a week, I was stabilized enough to be transferred to a rehabilitation facility closer to my home. There I was given a wheelchair for getting to the toilet by myself. Immediately I heard the devil whisper in my ear: "You are always going to be in this wheelchair." For someone who loves jogging, biking, and golf, that was not good news.

Fortunately I was blessed enough to also hear Father God say something—something that he had spoken into my mind many times over the past 23 years: "Remember, Fred, I have told you that my hand is upon you for the good."

As I listened to the two voices in my head, I knew I had a choice to make. Just which voice was I going to believe?

At that point, I thanked God for his reminder and the lie from the devil disappeared from my mind. Thanksgiving began to take over in my life. I would wake up in the hospital and thank God that I was alive one more day, thank him that I was still here to love my wife, my two children, and our precious granddaughter. I began noticing that I was getting stronger and stronger, so I began thanking God for each step forward in my recovery, no matter how little.

Within a week, my physical therapist took away the wheelchair and gave me a cane to use to get to the toilet. I thanked God for this progress and received it as a gift from him. Thanksgiving was becoming a lifestyle for me again.

Soon I was jogging between the parallel bars in the physical therapy room. Then after three weeks, I was released from the rehabilitation center to my home. There I had to negotiate the seventeen stairs up to my bedroom. No problem!! The doctors at the rehabilitation center had strongly suggested that we sell our townhouse because of those seventeen stairs between each of our three floors, but it was not necessary.

ADDING REST TO THANKFULNESS

My roommate at the rehabilitation center, a Presbyterian pastor who was also recuperating from a stroke, told me that his brother, who did stroke research, was convinced that rest was imperative for stroke patients' recoveries. Knowing that continued rest would play a big part in my return to health, my wife and I went to Myrtle Beach, South Carolina, where we stayed in the beach home of some friends for a month.

The beach was an excellent place to jog, so after a few days, I began to jog about one mile a day. I was so grateful to be outside again and jogging that my thanksgiving increased. Then a next door neighbor loaned me a bike to use on the beach. Balance and visual acuity were required for dodging other beach visitors. I was thrilled and grateful once again to be regaining strength and balance. "THANK YOU, LORD, I CAN RIDE A BIKE!"

Though I made my wife more nervous, I began to ride the bike on the streets around our borrowed beach home, which meant using the added skill of monitoring traffic while maintaining balance. Each new step of progress I made, I received as a gift from God and said, "THANK YOU, FATHER!"

During our month stay in South Carolina, the pastor of the church we were attending there asked me to preach one Sunday. I told him he was taking a chance, because my thinking was still a bit garbled, but he didn't seem worried. Perhaps both of us took a deep breath, though, as I got up to speak, but the talk went well—well enough that he asked me if I could speak again. "THANK YOU, FATHER!" rang in my heart as I cleared that hurdle.

Upon returning to the Toronto area, I took up golf again, playing with some fellow pastors. Knowing that golf required complex physical coordination and mental calculations, I wondered that first time back on the course how well I would play. Much to my delight, my game had improved by fifteen strokes. I am still amazed and grateful for the return of that activity. "THANK YOU, FATHER!"

HEALING PRESERVED

I am convinced that thanksgiving facilitated and released much of my healing and helped maintain it. I encourage you to seek out more information about physical and emotional healing that comes through a response of thanksgiving during illnesses of any sort. We still have so much to learn about the effect of thanksgiving in the process of physical healing.

CHAPTER 8

THANKSGIVING, PROTECTING US FROM EMOTIONAL DISTRESS

Anxiety and other forms of emotional distress hit all of us. What varies is how we respond when they strike.

JONAH IN THE BELLY OF THE BIG FISH

The Old Testament prophet Jonah displayed an amazing response to panic, explored in Jonah 1:5–6. I can't imagine how desperate Jonah must have felt when he was thrown off a ship into the Mediterranean Sea during a life-threatening storm, and all because he had disobeyed God. Suddenly Jonah was facing terrors that he had brought upon himself.

His experience is described in Jonah 2:3, 5–6: *"The current engulfed me...Water encompassed me to the point of death...Weeds were wrapped around my head. I descended to the roots of the mountains."*

To top it all off, then he was swallowed by the monstrous fish and found himself in another horrific scene.

Jonah's response during this calamity was *todah*, a verbal sacrifice of thanksgiving made before being rescued. Such thanksgiving acknowledges who God is, without pleading for a particular outcome. Jonah did not beg God to rescue him; he just simply thanked him.

I don't believe Jonah gave thanks to manipulate God but to acknowledge that God is God, that God is good, and that his life was indeed in God's hands. Jonah's sacrifice of praise released God to respond with a miraculous rescue.

I believe thanksgiving warms the heart of the Lord. I think it does so because thanksgiving is the most basic expression of dependence on God and trust in him. Our utter desperation and dependency can become a basis for honoring God when they prompt thanksgiving, and that frees God to rescue us from emotional turmoil.

PAUL FINDS REST THROUGH THANKSGIVING

Another example that I want to share of rescue from distress is found in the New Testament. In 2 Corinthians 2:12–15, we see the Apostle Paul overcome by worry for his son in the Lord, Titus.

Paul had sent Titus to deliver the apostle's first letter to the church that had formed in Corinth. It was a very direct letter, confronting some major problems in that church. Paul had arranged to meet Titus in Troas after Titus had delivered the letter so Paul could learn how the Corinthian Christians had responded to it.

Paul writes in verse 12, *"Now when I came to Troas for the gospel of Christ and when a door was opened for me in the Lord ..."* giving the impression that the people in Troas were very open to the gospel. But Paul continues in verse 13, *"I had no rest for my spirit, not finding Titus my brother; but taking my leave of them, I went on to Macedonia."*

Paul was full of anguish because Titus had not arrived in Troas when expected. We can imagine the possible explanations for this that entered Paul's mind. What if the Corinthian church had turned on Titus after reading Paul's letter? What if Titus had been robbed, beaten, and left to die somewhere on his journey? Paul left a wide-open door of ministry in Troas to get on the road to find Titus.

Paul's tone suddenly changes in verse 14: *"But thanks be to God, who always leads us in triumph in Christ, and manifests through us the sweet aroma of the knowledge of Him in every place."*

What I sense here is that after Paul left Troas in a panic, the Holy Spirit reminded him to step back from his emotional state and seek God. As Paul began to listen for what God might want to say to him, he was rescued from worry. He remembered who his God was—the Good Shepherd, Light of the World, Savior of Mankind, Provider, Helper. He began to thank God for always leading him in triumph in Christ—he probably thanked God for also leading Titus in triumph in Christ—and his panic changed to trust and rest in the Lord. The sweet sense (the aroma) of knowing who God is began to permeate Paul's spirit and soul again.

THE WRIGHT SON FAILS
TO RETURN HOME IN TIME

I remember one night when my son, a teenager at the time, had not returned home by midnight as usual. I was very worried and could find no rest for my mind and heart. I couldn't get in touch with him, as he had no cell phone. Finally my wife told me to go to bed and that she would wait up for him.

She told me that as soon as I left the room and took the swirl of worry with me, she asked the Lord if she should be worried as well. The Lord told her, then, that Nathan was all right, so she waited in peace until he walked in the door at 4 AM.

During her hours of waiting, Sharon kept thanking God that Nathan was in his hands.

Nathan's delay was caused by circumstances beyond his control and he had no access to a phone to let us know what was happening. He was with a family waiting for their son in an empty parking lot. They also had no cell phone so their son could not phone them and tell them his predicament. It was one of those circus-like situations that drove us all to buying cell phones the next day.

So Sharon probably did what Paul did: inquired of the Lord about what was going on and she got the truth from him that she needed to keep her in peace.

SHARON ALSO MOANS

One day my wife was bemoaning a situation as she was talking on the phone with our daughter, Hanna, who was attending The School of the Miraculous in Redding, California. Hanna interrupted her with a stern admonition: "Mother, stop! I am going to get off the phone, and I want you to go into the front room with a pen and paper. Ask the Holy Spirit to come and show you all you have to be thankful for."

Sharon was caught up short and obeyed. The Holy Spirit came promptly, and she spent the next half hour scribbling as fast as she could all the things that he showed her that were worthy of thankfulness in her life. Her spiritual equilibrium was restored, and praise and worship were released, freeing her from her distress. It is a turnaround that she has never forgotten!

PILGRIMAGE

Psalm 84:5–7 describes the turnaround that can result when we rely on God while encountering the challenges of life:

> How blessed is the man whose strength is in You,
> In whose heart are the highways to Zion!
> Passing through the valley of Baca (the place of tears), they make it a spring;
> The early rain also covers it with blessings.
> They go from strength to strength.

"What are the highways to Zion?" I asked myself when I first read these verses.

Although I prefer to study from the New American Standard Bible, in this case the New International Version used phrasing that I understood better: *"Blessed are those ... whose hearts are set on pilgrimage."* So *"highways to Zion,"* or highways to the place where God dwells in intimate relationship with his people, is a metaphor for a process, a journey, not an end destination.

We can rest in the fact that we are on our way from point A to point B. Even if our current place is the valley of Baca, a place of tears, it is not the whole story of our lives! No matter what today looks like, what next week looks like, what even the upcoming year looks like, we are on a pilgrimage with our God and he is completely trustworthy. When we turn our thoughts to God and his goodness and his faithfulness as we have seen them manifested in our past, or in the pasts of others such as Jonah and Paul, any circumstance, any valley of tears, can become a place of springs with living water.

We do not say this lightly. We have walked through dismissal from the church in Seaside, California. We have lived through the sudden death of two siblings and the deaths of our parents. We have lived through the crib death of our seven-week-old son. We have lived through the loss of reputation and friends as we began to walk with the Holy Spirit. We have lived through ridicule as we joined the team at the church in Toronto where the "Father's Blessing" revival broke out in 1994. I have had a stroke, a *grand mal* seizure that set me aside for three days, and prostate cancer.

What has steadied us and taken us from "strength to strength" is thanking God, and knowing the God we thank.

WE ALL NEED TO KNOW WHO OUR GOD IS

Philippians 3:10 says, *"that I may know Him and the power of His resurrection and the fellowship of His sufferings."* As in human relationships, real "knowing" of God, real intimacy with him, requires walking with him through every circumstance.

It is so important to continually discover who he is by also reading about him in the Bible; by fellowshipping with the community of believers; and receiving revelation from the Holy Spirit. Then when adversities come, thanksgiving to him is our natural response. When we know God, we can simply rest and trust in him, in his love for us, and in his plans for us.

"But God"—how we love that phrase in Scripture, which announces God's intervention in difficult situations. He has never abandoned us. He has comforted us and strengthened us. He has always been faithful to us as we have walked with him through every adversity.

WE DO NOT NEED TO LOSE HEART!

2 Corinthians 4:16–18 says:

> Therefore, we do not lose heart, but though our outer man is decaying, our inner man is being renewed day by day. For momentary, light affliction is producing for us an eternal weight of glory far beyond all comparison, while we look not at the things which are seen, but at the things which are not seen; for the things which are seen are temporal, but the things which are not seen are eternal.

When momentary, light afflictions come our way, most of us at first succumb to anxiety. Keeping our eyes on the unseen instead takes practice. Thanking God in every situation takes practice. Hearing his voice in our moments of panic takes practice.

Thanking God keeps us looking toward him, our ultimate source. Psalm 23 says he will restore our souls and guide us "in the paths of righteousness for his name's sake," and that "surely goodness and lovingkindness" will follow us all the days of our lives.

"THANK YOU, JESUS, FOR OVERCOMING THE WORLD AND LEADING US IN TRIUMPH IN CHRIST!"

CHAPTER 9

THANKSGIVING INHERENT IN THE GIFT OF TONGUES

Every spiritual gift listed in the New Testament has one or more purposes—and the gift of tongues is no less endowed. In fact, the gift of tongues has four clear purposes that we will briefly examine.

During the last century the gift of tongues has probably been one of the most controversial spiritual gifts. This probably came about because some well-meaning people within the Pentecostal movement taught that it was "THE SIGN" that a person had been baptized in the Holy Spirit. Some went so far as to say it was "THE SIGN" that a person even had the Holy Spirit. On the one hand, one can understand the delight that accompanied the outpouring of the Holy Spirit at Azusa Street Mission. Every time God pours himself out, much joy is released for those receiving and they want everyone else to be as delighted and to enter into their joy with them. On the other hand, the new or unusual manifestations that often accompany God's touch upon his people always cause consternation for those who aren't a part of the initial download.

The teaching on tongues being a sign gift created a great deal of controversy and ill will among Christians who had neither experience nor theology for it. In many cases this new outpouring from God divided and/or split churches. An even more unfortunate outcome is that it has kept a large section of the Body of Christ from even embracing the person, work and fullness of the Holy Spirit for today.

This has been a great disservice to God and to His purposes in and through believers. The purpose of this chapter is not to try to clear up this controversy once and for all, but to act like a "teaser" for your further exploration with the Father over the gift of tongues.

1 CORINTHIANS 14:
GOD'S TREASURE HUNT

1 Corinthians 14 is a treasure hunt that begins with this clear injunction in verse one: *"Pursue love, yet desire earnestly spiritual gifts ..."* The rest of this chapter lays out a mosaic of teaching about, and boundaries for, the use of the spiritual gifts of prophecy, tongues, the interpretation of tongues, and teaching. As Paul shares his heart, there are little nuggets about the gift of tongues woven in.

Even though Paul says in verse 5, *"I wish that you all spoke in tongues,"* you don't feel impugned if you don't. It is more like he is pointing out that this is something for you to discover and enjoy, but it is not the only gift in which you can participate. In fact, he goes on to say he would really rather that you prophesied, for it edifies the church.

So let us take a look at four interesting statements that Paul makes about this gift of tongues and how it fits into the bigger picture of church life and our personal, private walks with the Lord.

FOUR ASPECTS OF THE GIFT OF TONGUES

FIRST: 1 CORINTHIANS 14:22 SAYS: *"So then tongues are for a sign, not to those who believe but to unbelievers..."*

This is how the gift of tongues worked on the day that the church was born in Jerusalem, as told in the book of Acts in the New Testament. Having the gift of tongues helped the Galilean disciples to win over 3,000 unbelievers to the Lord as they spoke about the wonders of God and his gospel, not in their own tongue, but in the many tongues represented by the people present at the temple who had gathered to take part in the feast of Pentecost. The non-Christian Jews were astounded at the sign of hearing their own language coming out of the mouths of the men who didn't speak their language at all.

> And they were all filled with the Holy Spirit and began to speak with other tongues, as the Spirit was giving them utterance.
>
> Now there were Jews living in Jerusalem, devout men from every nation under heaven. And when this sound occurred, the crowd came together, and were bewildered because each one of them was hearing them speak in his own language. They were amazed and astonished saying, "Why, are not all these who are speaking Galileans? And how is it that we each hear them in our own language to which we were born? Parthians and Medes and Elamites, and residents of Mesopotamia...we hear them in our own tongues speaking of the mighty deeds of God." (Acts 2:4–11)

Speaking in tongues also became a sign to the apostles that the groups of people to whom they were ministering had really become believers. You need to remember that since they had been baptized in that way by the Spirit on the day of Pentecost, it was a confirmation to them as they began to go out and minister to Gentiles that God was doing the same thing in others as he had done in them. They needed all the signs from God that they could get to confirm to them that they were on the right track. So God gave them a sign that they understood:

> While Peter was still speaking these words, the Holy Spirit fell upon all those who were listening to the message. All the circumcised (*Jewish*) believers who came with Peter were amazed, because the gift of the Holy Spirit had been poured out on the Gentiles also. For they were hearing them speaking with tongues and exalting God. Then Peter answered, "Surely no one can refuse water for these to be baptized who have received the Holy Spirit just as we did, can he?" (Acts 10:44–47)

He (*Paul*) said to them, "Did you receive the Holy Spirit when you believed?" And they said to him, "No, we have not even heard whether there is a Holy Spirit." And he said, "Into what then were you baptized?" And they said, "John baptized with the baptism of repentance, telling the people to believe in Him who was coming after him, that is, Jesus." When they heard this, they were baptized in the name of the Lord Jesus. And when Paul had laid his hands upon them, the Holy Spirit came on them, and they began speaking with tongues and prophesying. (Acts 19:2–6)

SECOND: 1 Corinthians 14:4: "*One who speaks in a tongue edifies himself.*"

In verses 18–19, Paul says, "*I thank God I speak in tongues more than you all; however, in the church I desire to speak five words with my mind so that I may instruct others also, rather than ten thousand in a tongue.*"

Speaking in tongues appears to be the only gift that does not really need other people around to fulfill its purposes. What we could perhaps glean from 1 Corinthians 14:18–19 is that for Paul, tongues was primarily used in his personal prayer life.

Why did that come about in Paul's life? We know from Scripture that once Paul became a Christian he got involved in mission work, making three arduous mission journeys that are recorded in the book of Acts in the New Testament. He spent much of his time alone on these journeys, being accompanied often by only one other man. Those journeys were not as easy as stepping on a plane or getting in a car today like the many itinerant ministers of our age do.

And once he got to a place, he never knew what his reception would be. He had a history of being stoned and left for dead, put in prison, etc. It sounds like his experience of speaking in tongues built him up in the inner man as he went on these journeys. As he spoke in tongues, he felt encouraged, and, of course, he would be sensing the Holy Spirit's fullness continually in this way.

THIRD: 1 Corinthians 14:14-15 says, "*For if I pray in a tongue, my spirit prays, but my mind is unfruitful. What is the outcome then? I will pray with the spirit and I will pray with the mind also; I will sing with the spirit and I will sing with the mind also.*"

In verse 14, it states that the mind is unfruitful while speaking in tongues. This simply means that the mind is not the power behind the activity of speaking in tongues, but rather the Holy Spirit is the power behind it and flowing through the person thus engaged. Because speaking in tongues does not engage the mind but is done by being engaged in the Spirit's flow, it is possible to pray without ceasing even when engaged in other tasks. Thus, Paul's injunction in 1 Thessalonians 5:17, *"Pray without ceasing,"* becomes possible.

Prayer is one of the important purposes for speaking in tongues. In Ephesians 6:18, Paul commands the Ephesian Christians, *"With all prayer and petition pray at all times in the Spirit..."* I believe that this praying in the Spirit is praying in tongues—which allows the Holy Spirit to intercede for those specific things needing prayer at any given time, even things we have no knowledge of.

FOURTH: 1 Corinthians 14:16–17 says, *"Otherwise if you bless in the spirit only, how will the one who fills the place of the ungifted say the 'Amen' at your giving of thanks, since he does not know what you are saying? For you are giving thanks well enough ..."*

In these two verses Paul sneaks in the fact that when you are speaking in tongues, you are blessing and giving thanks. Those around you may not discern that unless God gives them the interpretation, but part of what is going on while you are speaking in tongues is thanksgiving empowered by the Holy Spirit.

This makes it possible to fulfill the injunction in 1 Thessalonians 5:18: *"... in everything give thanks; for this is God's will for you in Christ Jesus."*

"THANK YOU, JESUS FOR MAKING THE GIFT OF TONGUES AVAILABLE TO US SO WE CAN PRAY AND WALK IN THANKFULNESS ALL THE TIME."

CHAPTER 10

THE DANGER OF LOSING
A THANKFUL HEART

Having looked at the beneficial effects of thanksgiving to God, I would like to look at the other side of the equation—what happens when people lose the attitude and practice of turning to God with thanksgiving in their hearts and on their lips.

GOD IS...

In the letter to the Romans in the New Testament, the Apostle Paul gives an excellent exposition of the good news of the gospel of Jesus Christ to the new believers in Rome. These new believers have lived for most of their lives under the domination of Rome—with all its depravity and countless pagan gods. But before he teaches in depth on the salvation given to men through Jesus Christ's death and resurrection, he shares the amazing truth that before Jesus came to earth to be a demonstration of God the Father's love and power and person, there was an even earlier and obvious witness given to men that God is the one back of the creation of the earth.

Paul writes in Romans 1:19–20, "*...because that which is known about God is evident within them; for God made it evident to them. For since the creation of the world, His invisible attributes, His eternal power and divine nature, have been clearly seen, being understood through what has been made, so that they are without excuse.*"

Sharon's mother echoed that thought on the simplest level. Although this woman didn't go to church for many years, she would often say as her gaze rested on the foothills surrounding her small hometown in Northern California: "There must be a God. Look at the mountains!"

A similar innate sense that there is someone back of the universe is found in many primitive tribes, even those living far away from the western lands where the truth of God has been deposited through the centuries of preaching and teaching about Him and His plan of salvation through His Son, Jesus.

In their inner beings there is a "knowing" that there has to be someone behind the universe with a plan, someone who is bigger than they are and has more power than they do. They may not be able to describe that someone or his plan as those of us who have been raised in the western nations where salvation has been preached, but they can see that there is a higher power that has to be acknowledged in some way. Often they designate some powerful force in nature, i.e., the sun, moon, stars, thunder, etc., as their god, since whatever they have chosen demonstrates to them the most power.

There are many missionary stories told of whole tribes coming to the salvation available in Jesus once the truth is told to them about who God is and about his plan for salvation and relationship with them.

THE ADVENTURE OF
REALLY LOOKING AT NATURE

I know, myself, that when I am out in creation, I see demonstrations of God's power and person everywhere. It has become an adventure to decipher what God might be trying to reveal about Himself through different aspects of His creation.

I won't go into all of my discoveries, but in the relentless, pounding waves of the ocean I see demonstrations of His power and unceasing activity. The delicate and colorful mountain flowers, not seen by many but the most ardent hikers in tundra areas, point to his love of detail and beauty in every part of the "home" he created for man. On my last trip to Alaska, I drove around a corner to be confronted with a valley full of spruce trees, all lifting their branches towards heaven. I felt like they must be prophesying: "Look up, look up to see the King of Kings and Lord of Lords."

I even heard the story of an atheist watching a sunset on an evening stroll. The beauty that he saw overwhelmed him and touched him so deeply that he cried out spontaneously, "Thank you, thank you!" When he got back home, he relayed his experience to his wife.

Her comment was: "You are an atheist! Who were you thanking?" He was caught off guard by her very insightful question and had to think through his own reaction to the beauty of creation.

THE BIBLICAL PERSPECTIVE
IN ROMANS 1:21, 28–32

Paul writes in Romans 1:21: "*For even though they knew God, they did not honor Him as God or* **give thanks**, *but they became futile in their speculations, and their foolish heart was darkened.*"

As I read this, I wondered which voice this Greek verb, "was darkened", was in. I had to study Greek in seminary and there I learned that the verb structure can be very helpful in understanding what is being said by the writers in the New

Testament. As I read my *Interlinear Greek Bible*, I found out that "was darkened" is in the passive voice, meaning that these people who did not honor God nor thank him gave unseen permission for their minds to be darkened by something, some force, outside themselves.

I was also curious about what "darkened" meant so I opened my study tool, *The Expository Dictionary of New Testament Words* by W.E. Vine, which I keep handy as I am reading the Bible. There I read that the word 'darkened' comes from the Greek word *skoteinos*, "full of darkness". Vine also wrote that *skoteinos* and all the other "*skot*" words are derived from a root *ska--*, meaning to cover. (The same root is to be found in *skene*, a tent.) The picture comes to mind of someone pulling a blanket over their minds to keep out the truth, perhaps even to hide from the truth.

Paul expands this thought at the end of chapter one, in verses 28–32:

> And just as they did not see fit to acknowledge God any longer, *God gave them over to a depraved mind*, to do those things which are not proper, being filled with all unrighteousness, wickedness, greed, evil; full of envy, murder, strife, deceit, malice; they are gossips, slanderers, haters of God, insolent, arrogant, boastful, inventors of evil, disobedient to parents, without understanding, untrustworthy, unloving, unmerciful; and although they know the ordinance of God, that those who practice such things are worthy of death, they not only do the same, but also give hearty approval to those who practice them.

JUST WHAT IS A DEPRAVED MIND?

The Greek word that is translated in the New American Standard Bible as "**depraved**" and in the King James version of the Bible as "**reprobate**" mind is *adokimos*, signifying "not standing the test", "rejected". The Greeks applied this word to metals primarily that did not stand up to the test that they were put under to prove what they were.

I then went to *The Oxford Concise English Dictionary* where the word depraved is defined as "led away from what is natural or right; corrupt". In the Middle English, *depraver*, means to "pervert in meaning or intention".

Just that little bit of study points to the fact that when we do not see fit to acknowledge God any longer, to dishonor him, to stop thanking him, we become less than, or other than, what we were created to be. Our minds begin to lead us away from what is natural or right.

OUR CHOICE

What did I glean from this study? There is a choice always before us as human beings. We can acknowledge God as God and respond with thanksgiving as we pursue even more revelation, understanding, and knowledge of him, or we can ignore the truth before us in creation and in the historical witness of Jesus' life, death and resurrection here on earth. We can embrace God's revelation and truth or cover our minds from receiving His truth.

If we ignore the witness of God which is inherent in creation because the idea of being related to him is an offense to our sense of being in control of our own destinies or because things do not always make sense to our natural minds, God finally responds by giving us over to the mindset we choose, and our minds begin to be darkened as we wander away from the truth about him (Romans 1:21).

The bigger cosmic picture here, of God letting us have our own way, giving us free will to even choose things that will harm us, can be seen in the modest earthly picture of the frustrated and beleaguered parents of a teenager!

Often teenagers, with their lack of wisdom, will not agree with the rules and boundaries put in place by their parents. They do not see why the parents would say, "No!" to what seems to them to be harmless activities in their eagerness to experience things with their equally-clueless friends. As the parents struggle to lead and guide their children through the teen years with wisdom, they often discover what their kids have been doing despite their parental guidance. These parents throw up their hands in despair, realizing that there is nothing that they can do or say that will influence their children. In their despair, they may just give up even trying.

With God the Father, there is also a giving over of us to our depraved and darkened minds to do what we want to do even when he knows we will harm ourselves. He says in effect, "Do what you want to do," even though he knows that we will be stepping away from what we were created to be and do, having life-giving relationship with him.

He finally gives us over to our depraved thinking. He is offering us life, love, salvation, truth, hope, but if we keep running from that in an effort to deify/glorify our minds and our perceptions apart from him, he finally gives us over to 'corrupt' thinking.

It is not a pretty picture as you read Romans 1:28–32 and it is beyond the scope of this book to examine the details of this passage or to trace the progression of moral decay that is presented in these verses. But we can point out one more time the very first factors that begin the slippery decline down the slope of a depraved mind: "...*although they knew God, they did not glorify Him as God, nor were they thankful.*" The response of a grateful heart in pouring out thanksgiving to God, the Father, is a safeguard for us all.

EVEN CHRISTIANS...

Two points are worth noting here:

FIRST: The steps on the downward, dismal slope into spiritual darkness are steps that can be taken even by those who know God and who have established a relationship with him. Many of us who are "long-term" believers can testify to times or even seasons in our lives when the keen edge of profound intimacy with God was diminished, even lost. During those times, we still might identify ourselves as God's children but we lose our grip on the truths about God and the truths about ourselves. Our circumstances seem dark and heavy. We can no longer see His goodness or kindness and we stop reaching out for him and for his help. We may even turn our backs on him for a while. It is easy to stop giving thanks during those times!

Circumstances are the perfect breeding ground for either thanksgiving and praise or for self-pity, anger, resentment, and bitterness. It is interesting to note in the story of Job, that his wife's reaction to the all-encompassing calamities they were experiencing as a family, including the death of their children, loss of their wealth, and then chronic bodily pain on Job's part, was: "Do you still hold on to your integrity? Curse God and die!"

And Job's reaction? *"You speak as one of the foolish women speaks. Shall we indeed accept good from God and not accept adversity?"* (Job 2:9–10) Job seemed to understand that both God's kindness and the world's calamities are ever-present in a fallen world, that tribulations cannot be avoided in such a context—and that somehow God is still on the throne and has answers for us.

Job could see beyond the circumstances and still worship God, still turn towards him. He was looking beyond his circumstances to keep a hold on his God. His understanding was being stretched and although that was a painful process, he kept his eyes on his God!

SECOND: The issue is not only the evil that is done, but also the good that is not done. This means that maintaining life-giving connection with our heavenly Father involves not merely abstaining from certain actions and attitudes, but also positively cultivating vital states of heart and mind, namely worship, "glorifying" Him as God, and thankfulness. If we do nothing to continually build relationship with God, the subtle forces of spiritual erosion can begin to affect us, perhaps in such seemingly insignificant increments that only after a time will the cumulative effect become noticeable.

So the choice we make to find God in every situation and give him thanks is a definite action of mind, spirit, heart and tongue. Neglecting to give thanks, not finding reasons to give him thanks, can be our downfall into negativity.

I believe Paul would encourage us as God's children to be careful, not only to thank him for the obvious things he has given us, but also to thank him in advance by faith for the things that he has made available to us and for us that we have not yet received or experienced.

FINISHING WELL

My dream about thanksgiving came during a very difficult transition in my life. It was easy to only see what was being taken away—and then only a few months later, I was hit with a stroke that left me unable to talk, think, walk, or move in any way. The reminder from God through the dream of the jolly monks was the perfect preparation for going through an adverse time with the Lord. I had been given the admonition to return to thankfulness, which had diminished in my life due to distractions on many levels, and now I had plenty of time while recovering from the stroke to put thanksgiving into practice.

There is a desire in all of us to finish well. Continual, daily thanksgiving to our God from a heart trained in being thankful keeps us going towards him even when the 'going gets rough.' As we thank him, our minds will continually be transformed and enlightened and infused with God's truths and purposes—and our thanksgiving and trust in him and his goodness will grow by leaps and bounds.

CHAPTER 11

THE GREATEST MAN
I HAVE KNOWN

I have recently been thinking a lot about the heritage we leave when we pass on. This probably has to do with my age and with my experience of watching a few close friends and some family members go on to be with the Lord before me in the past decade.

This whole process of thinking about how many of these people have affected my life has caused me to reflect on many of the well-known Christians with whom God has graced my path over the years and the privilege it has been to receive important deposits of the kingdom of God from them.

I am very grateful for the extended periods of time I have had with people like Jack Hamilton, William C. Thomas, Major Ian Thomas, Roger and Faith Forster, John Wimber, John and Carol Arnott, Heidi and Rolland Baker, and Bill Johnson.

These men and women of God have shared wisdom with me, prayed for me, rebuked me at times, and in general encouraged me to go deeper into God. They have played invaluable roles in my life and I am grateful to each one of them.

Because of many of them would be considered as apostles of the faith by many, and some of them will probably attain historic stature as well, many of you might wonder why I have been so blessed. I know that I am grateful to have received from them. However, in my lifetime, the one person I feel most privileged to have known and to have been impacted by is Estes Wright, my earthly father.

He was not the founder of any movement; he would not be listed in anyone's book as an apostle or large-church pastor. I never heard him teach or preach the Bible. But in my book he is the greatest on the list because he knew how to humbly serve his wife, family and Lord, walking in thankfulness, which was the heart attitude of his life. As he walked in thankfulness, it affected all those around him, including me. If I were to write an epitaph for his life it would be: "He Walked in Thankfulness, Which Changed My Life."

Many times it is the stories that are told about you by others that mean you have left a mark on the world. So here is the story about my father, Estes Wright, a man who left much fruit behind. His early childhood years were full of trauma, yet he was not disposed to moaning over his circumstances. He had very little in the way of worldly goods, and he had no sense of entitlement. He was able to live in contentment with what he had. He was able to "see" what he had and was deeply thankful to God for it.

A TRAUMATIC START

Estes, the first of three children, was four years old when his mother died of tuberculosis. His father was so overcome with grief when she died that he didn't feel capable of caring for his three children by himself. So he sent them to live with their grandfather, who was a dryland farmer in eastern New Mexico. The grandfather struggled with a heart condition, so much of Estes' early years included caring for his two sisters and himself, as well as doing what he could to help his grandfather on the farm.

But the children were together and not split up among different family members, something for which my dad was very thankful.

About the time Estes turned ten, his father remarried and felt stable enough to have the three children come back to live with him and his new family. At nearly the same time the three siblings were returning to live in their father's household, the grandfather died of a ruptured appendix so once again they were touched by death.

Soon after their arrival in the home of their father, a new sibling was born to him and their new stepmother. Then tragedy struck again within a few months, just as they were all getting acquainted, Estes' father died of pneumonia.

The new stepmother was so overwhelmed with the death of her husband that she felt caring for four children on her own was beyond her physical and emotional strength. She tried to find someone in the family who could take in all three of the older children so they could be together in their grief. The traumatized siblings couldn't bear to be separated. But it seemed the only alternative was that they go to three different homes.

Finally, a decision was made by Estes, only ten years old—the three would go together to the Buckner Orphans Home, in Dallas, Texas. All three were deeply grieving as they settled in, but they were thankful that they would be cared for and could be together.

JESUS ENTERS AN ORPHAN'S WORLD

After supper in the evenings, the three siblings would huddle together, grief-stricken, on the front steps of the Home's dining room. One of the women teachers noticed them in tears there and took a deep interest in them. She spent time with them—enough time to lead Estes into a personal relationship with Jesus Christ. My dad told me that this made all the difference in the world, because Jesus became a comforter for him. Having Jesus as his Savior also gave my father incentive to work hard, study hard, and get involved in sports.

When my father became a bit older, he started playing American football on the Buckner Orphan Home's high school team. Because the team was so small, he played both offensive and defensive positions, although he weighed only about 120 pounds. The team's uniforms, he told me, consisted of old sweatshirts with crudely-fashioned numbers sewn on by the girls in the school. The team had helmets but no shoulder or hip pads like those worn by their opponents.

The Orphanage campus didn't have room for a football field with bleachers for spectators, so all of the team's games were played away. An old bus carried the team to the games, but the Home had no transportation for the team's supporters. So at every game, as my dad and his teammates entered the field, one side was full of parents and students cheering for their opponents, while the Buckner Orphans Home side was empty and silent. Yet, my dad said, he was thankful that he could play football because it was a diversion from his grief, hard studies and work assignments at the orphanage.

Thankfulness in the midst of a bleak situation got seeded into my father's life during those orphanage days, and it remained rooted and flowing in him until he died at the age of 88.

After graduating from high school, Estes could no longer stay at the orphanage. He slowly made his way through a two-year community college course in eastern New Mexico, and then headed to New Mexico State College, in Las Cruces, where he studied electrical engineering. He worked his way through university at various jobs, including haircutting, earning a Bachelor of Science degree without incurring student debts. He was thankful for all of God's provision.

FINDING THE LOVE OF HIS LIFE

While he was studying to be an electrical engineer, my father Estes met my mother, Evelyn, the daughter of Swedish immigrants who were farmers. They fell in love almost immediately. She was the second of four children, so when my father visited her home, he experienced what it was like to be a part of a real family.

He had a hard time winning over Evelyn's parents, however. The blond-haired, blue-eyed Swedes were suspicious of a black-haired, black-eyed man with an olive complexion, but they finally succumbed to his kind ways and his obvious love for God and their daughter.

My mom and dad remained deeply in love and stayed committed to each other for more than sixty years. Throughout their long marriage, my father was thankful for his loving wife, who bore him five children, of which I was the first.

Our family never had much materially because my dad was not paid much for helping to pioneer the Moody Institute of Science, then a fledgling ministry born out of the Chicago-based Moody Bible Institute. The science institute, located in the Los Angeles area, developed a series of science-based evangelistic films that were used for many years worldwide; these continue to be a resource today for science teachers in elementary schools.

My siblings and I saw how dependent my parents were on God, even to feed us. Yet we were not subject to moaning about what we didn't have or couldn't afford. Instead, there was a sense of looking to God for provision and help in time of need, and we saw God's provision in our home over and over again.

My dad looked at everything he had as a gift from his loving Father God, and he sowed into his family thankfulness for God's provision and guidance. As I reflect on the many wonderful qualities in my dad, his thankfulness stands out the most.

DISCOVERIES ABOUT THE FAMILY LINE

Sometime in his late sixties, my dad decided to take my mom on a vacation to visit his family. He had very little information about his mother's branch of the family tree, so first they visited his aunts, uncles and cousins on his father's side. My dad began to find out from them a bit more about his mother's line.

As they made stop after stop on this trip throughout New Mexico and eventually Arkansas, my dad discovered that his mother's heritage was Cherokee Indian and that his grandparents on her side had been Methodist evangelists among the Cherokees. No wonder he had olive-colored skin, dark hair and eyes!

CELEBRATING A BIRTHDAY, A FAMILY

When my dad turned seventy years old, his extended family and friends threw him a surprise birthday party. At one point during the festivities, he was handed a microphone and was asked to share about his life. I will never forget how he took a few moments before he started speaking to look at each person there. Then he said to all those sixty-five people or so assembled, with tears in his eyes, "Do you know that I always just wanted a family?" He publicly gave thanks then for his wife and to each one present for coming to celebrate with him and being the family he had yearned to have.

THE FRUIT OF MY FATHER'S THANKFUL LIFE

My dad modeled thankfulness and sowed it into his family throughout his life. He also sowed into his children his pioneering spirit that asked in the face of any difficulty, "What can be done in this situation?" That, too, included thankfulness, as my dad acknowledged his dependency on God and thanked him for his continual aid. I believe that the thankfulness and the pioneering spirit that my dad sowed into his five children have played a significant role in each of us becoming people who have served our churches and communities. Our activities are part of the fruit of my father's thankful life:

I have held leadership roles since my youth, including in college as club director at 15 high school campuses for Youth for Christ in the Los Angeles area; helped found the Bible school in Sweden while serving with what is now Torchbearers International; pastored several churches, including two that I planted; and helped found and lead Partners in Harvest, the international fellowship of churches and ministries that grew out of the "Father's Blessing" revival in Toronto.

My parents' second child, Sigrid, and her husband, a Dutchman, ministered through Dutch Christian television in the

Netherlands for several years before she died after giving birth to her fourth daughter.

My parents' third child, Milton, has been a champion of the disabled. He founded a company/charity that helped those with disabilities enter the workforce, and has successfully worked through governmental channels to get wheelchair ramps and other structural adaptations legislated and built for them. He is now vice chairman of the California State Rehabilitation Council.

The fourth child, Steve, served as a criminal defense attorney for many years, committing himself to making sure the prosecution truly proved its case and also doing pro bono work to ensure fair trials. More than fifteen hundred people came to his memorial service in 2011, when many honored him for being a loving father figure to them as they worked through their personal difficulties.

The fifth child, Jeannie, and her husband have pastored churches for many years and are now are pastoring a motorcycle group in the Pacific Northwest, the Black Sheep Harley Davidsons for Christ.

THANKFUL EVEN ON HIS DEATHBED

At the end of his life, my father told the nine or so family members gathered around his hospital bed that he felt like he was the richest man in the world because of his family and his relationship with Jesus. He had started in life with almost nothing, but he finished his life wealthy in love, in family, and in opportunities to reflect the love of Father God.

On his deathbed, surrounded by family members and wearing an oxygen mask, my father talked by phone to nineteen other family members or friends who couldn't be at his bed-side. He told them he loved them and how thankful he was for them and the part they had played in his life. Then he prayed over them until his breathing stopped and he went home to be with the Lord.

He was totally thankful to the end.

CHAPTER 12

CULTIVATING A CULTURE OF THANKSGIVING

Danny Silk, on the Senior Management Team at Bethel Church in Redding, California, teaches about a "culture of honor." One aspect of this teaching is about honoring others with our words, learning how to encourage others by letting them know how much God appreciates them and how much we appreciate them. Ideally, it would become our nature to see the current capacity and the amazing potential of each person we meet and convey that honoring heart toward them.

When our daughter, Hanna, was attending one of Bethel's schools in Redding, we visited her there and noticed that the school building was reverberating with the compliment, "You are awesome!" The students were putting into practice honoring everyone they bumped into.

During one visit we took Sharon's mother, who was in her early nineties at the time. As she walked down the hallways, students who knew our daughter would gather around this fragile, silver-haired woman and tell her how awesome she was. Her response probably wasn't what the students expected. She wasn't able to connect much with their affirmation.

As I reflected on that, I realized that Sharon's mom had no relationship with any of these people, so their words had no shared experience to be connected to. Honoring people is best done when the hearts are connected with some type of history between those involved.

THANKSGIVING RELEASED INTO SOCIETY

As God began to re-establish thanksgiving in me, my heart began to see how many people serve me in society who get little or no honor in the form of thanks, other than a paycheck at the end of the month.

I also remembered how my dad and mom had instilled in me the practice of expressing thanks. When I was a boy, I was told before I attended a birthday party of a friend to remember to thank the parents before I came home for inviting me and for the good time that I had had. When our family was invited to someone else's home for dinner, I was told to thank the hosts before leaving for the good food and the lovely evening.

So I started being more deliberate about extending my thanksgiving toward others in everyday life. I thanked servers in restaurants, along with leaving them generous tips. As I got off airplanes, I thanked the flight attendants and I thanked the pilots, if they were standing alongside the flight attendants. I thanked the checkout clerks in grocery stores, the doctors and nurses who gave me medical care, my pastor for his sermons, my wife for her many acts of service to me, and others on this ongoing list.

Often I would ask God to bring to mind something specific for which I could thank each person, so that my thanksgiving was not just done out of a compulsory habit but had content. Once, as Sharon and I were walking through a department store, I thanked a clerk for the smile she bestowed upon us. It had certainly brightened my day.

Several people, when I've thanked them, have responded with surprise: "No one has ever thanked me before!" or "That made my day!"

Offering thanksgiving in society counters the culture of entitlement that has been growing among us, the culture that says, "I deserve good service!" or "The world owes me a living, and a good one at that!" It fosters a positive culture.

AN EYE-OPENING VACATION EXPERIENCE

Years ago my family and I were heading home from a vacation in the Rocky Mountains when we witnessed an eye-opening expression of thanksgiving within a culture.

Our return trip took us through Cody, Wyoming, just as a Native American family was hosting a major celebration in a big tent at the fairgrounds. The family was honoring a son who had qualified for the US Olympic wrestling team, publicly thanking and honoring all those who had played a significant role in his life, including his first-grade teacher, his high school and college wrestling coaches, and the tribal chief. As part of the celebration, the family gave significant gifts to those they were thanking—a beautiful feathered war bonnet, what looked like a Hudson's Bay wool trade blanket, and a beautiful beaded choker necklace among them.

We were told that the Native American concept of wealth differs from ours. Wealth in that culture is not seen as what a person accumulates for himself, but as what a person has beyond the essentials he or she needs that can be given away to honor others.

Our family was touched by what we saw and heard. I had just recently learned about my Cherokee heritage, so I was inspired to embrace this Native American perspective and give from my family's resources in a greater way.

On my fiftieth and sixtieth birthdays, the friends I invited to my home received gifts from our accumulated treasures to honor the parts they had played in my life. I did not choose items of little value to me to clear out my home, but things that cost me to give away.

A QUESTION TO PONDER

Could we really take thanksgiving to a level that begins to powerfully affect those around us? I know that the jolly monks in my dream significantly affected me as I saw their thankful approach to daily life. They reignited thanksgiving in my heart.

Opening our hearts to thanking God helps open our eyes to seeing beyond just the physical world around us. With eyes wide open to God's provision on every level, we can afford to extend our thankfulness to others for their parts, however small, in our lives.

Thanksgiving, as it grows in us, flows two ways, both vertically to God and horizontally towards those around us. Hearts that are grateful just seem to have an overflow that splashes onto everyone that they come into contact with.

We could compare it to the two great commandments that Jesus summarized for the Pharisees in Matthew 22:37–39:

> "'You shall love the Lord your God with all your heart, and with all your soul, and with all your mind.' This is the great and foremost commandment. The second is like it, 'You shall love your neighbor as yourself.'"

Thanksgiving, like love, is meant to be expressed both vertically and horizontally—toward God and then toward the world around us—one person at a time.

And in that way, we create a culture of thanksgiving that connects people heart to heart.

CHAPTER 13

THANKSGIVING, THE SOURCE OF TRUE REST IN ANY AGE

This is both an exhilarating and a potentially overwhelming age to be alive!

The exhilarating part for those of us who know Jesus Christ as our Savior is that many of the signs Jesus mentioned in Matthew 24:4–14 and Luke 21:8–28 are beginning to become a reality right before our eyes, in fact they could be today's headlines:

"Nation Rises Against Nation!"
"Famines!"
"Earthquakes!"
"Lawlessness Increasing! "
"Plagues!"

It would be a good idea for you to read through these two passages to see the information that Jesus considered was important for us to know about the end of the age. The conclusion by Luke, after listing many of the hard things inherent to the end of the age, is, *"But when these things begin to take place, straighten up and lift up your heads, because your redemption is drawing near."* (Luke 21:28)

There is a growing realization across the Body of Christ that the second coming of Jesus Christ is closer than ever before. We just might be in the generation that *"...will see the Son of Man coming in a cloud with power and great glory."* (v. 27)

The potentially overwhelming aspect of this turbulent time is already reflected in today's newspaper headlines and over-heard on newscasters' reports. Reports on wars and rumors of war, not to mention the strained situation of the global economy, are enough to distract and trouble anyone. But we don't want to be among those who will be *"fainting from fear and the expectation of the things which are coming upon the world."* (v. 26)

TO BE EATEN...OR NOT

Sharon found that her introduction to Christianity included a wake-up call. Part of the curriculum of the Capernwray Bible School we attended in the fall of 1962 included some required reading. One of those required books was *Foxes' Book of Martyrs*. It described all sorts of torture that Christians throughout many centuries had experienced at the hands of those antagonistic to the gospel of Jesus Christ.

She told me that she began wondering if she would have been able to face the same situations without running or deny-ing Christ, as had the courageous Christians in those seasons of history. As she was exploring her own inner strength to face being eaten by lions like the early Christians, she heard God say: "Sharon, I only give you the grace that you need for today. I will not give you the grace to be fed to lions today since that is not what will be happening to you today."

She was able then to relax and concentrate on her studies and God did give her the grace to do that. Today, most of us don't need the grace to face all of the things we read about in those two passages about the end times. We just need the grace to live our lives and go to work full of the Holy Spirit.

So in the midst of these times we live in, we only need to

find the grace for TODAY and the circumstances that come with it. We don't need to be people 'fainting over their expectations' of the things to come.

THE CRUX OF THE MATTER

So we have a choice set before us: what and who will we believe in and follow TODAY as well as during the days to come? Obviously, it is easier to follow someone you know and trust! So how does trust get built in us?

We usually learn to trust someone by walking along-side them, acquiring a history of events and situations that demonstrate who they really are—their character—and how they act in any given situation.

So how do we get to the place that Paul did, where he could say, *"But thanks be to God, who always leads us in triumph in Christ, and manifests through us the sweet aroma of the knowledge of Him in every place"*? (2 Corinthians 2:14) That proclamation was backed up by his history of walking with God. All he had to do was think about his years of walking with the Lord to see God's faithfulness and goodness. It hadn't been without pressure or tribulation, but God had saved him out of it all to live another day.

THAT I MAY KNOW HIM

Thanksgiving to God for always leading us in the triumph of Christ is an amazing key to living the Christian life, but it is ultimately linked with the other key thought in that verse: *"the sweet aroma of the knowledge of Him in every place."*

Knowing God was what life was all about to Paul. In Philippians 3:10 he writes: *"...that I may know Him and the power of His resurrection and the fellowship of His sufferings, being conformed to his death."* The Greek word, both for "**the knowledge of Him** in every place" and "**know** Him", *ginosko*, means:

> to be taking in knowledge,
>
> to come to know, recognize and understand,
>
> to understand completely.

Paul didn't seem to care whether he was going to be experiencing the resurrection power of God in every situation or suffering somewhere—like in the day he and Silas had both been beaten with rods as a punishment for delivering a slave girl from the spirit that made it possible for her to tell fortunes. (You can read about that story in Acts 16:14–24.)

Paul just wanted to keep pressing into God, and he knew that every situation was an opportunity to see God in action and get to experience him, get to have a new revelation about him. He also got to experience God's comfort, or strengthening, so that he could go on when the situation was tough. No wonder this man could thank God in everything. Paul could thank God for leading him in triumph in Jesus.

Paul understood the marvelous interplay between our getting to know God through our actual daily experiences with him.

OUR EXPERIENCES
WITH GOD DEEPEN OUR THANKSGIVING

So you and I also need to build a history of intimate knowledge of God, how God thinks and how God acts, who he is at the deepest levels of his magnificent being.

This intimate knowledge of God is gained in part through our daily experiences. As we see God acting on our behalf in difficult circumstances, we learn something more about him. Our knowledge of who God is grows and we become even more thankful that we belong to him and that we have a heavenly father who does make all things work together for good (Romans 8:28).

When we see God provide something we need, or pray for someone who needs physical healing and they get better, we suddenly know the miraculous power of God in a new arena. Pursuit of God in everyday life and through the circumstances in front of us reaps for us joy and peace and thankfulness beyond measure, because we always find him to be faithful and loving.

OUR OWN AWARENESS
OF THE FATHER HEART OF GOD DEEPENS

Sharon and I have learned that all things do work together for good. Even painful circumstances have been turned to gold in our lives as we find out where God is in them. Here is one we are sharing because the circumstances didn't change; but the very circumstances that were so painful brought with them, as we walked through the process, some knowledge about God that has blessed our lives ever since.

It started as Sharon went in to feed our seven-week old son one morning and found that he had died sometime during the night. He was still a bit warm, but she could tell that Joshua was no longer with us. We later learned he had died of "crib death." She cried out to God in her pain, saying, "God, I cannot do this!"

Calling out to God in her pain brought him right alongside in the person of the Holy Spirit, who began to give her truth to sustain her during this unexpected and traumatic circumstance.

First of all, she heard God say: "I have not taken your son; but I have received your son." Immediately all the lies that Satan wanted to pour into her heart about God punishing her for some sin fell to the ground. It also eliminated any chance for Satan to give God the false reputation as the author of death.

Then she was given a peek into heaven to see what was happening at that moment: she saw Joshua in God's hands. He was holding Joshua in the same position that I had held my son each night before we put him down to sleep. When I was holding him, he would stare up at me with eyes not quite able to focus yet, and his little head would wobble a bit from side to side on a still-new neck with weak and untrained muscles.

In contrast to what Joshua had been able to see here on earth, Joshua's face in the vision, as he looked into the face of God, had two very wide-opened eyes, full of awestruck wonder. God then said to Sharon, "Joshua is seeing things you long to see! Do you really want to call him back to earth with all its fallenness: broken relationships, lost jobs, illnesses?"

Sharon's answer was a simple "No! You keep him."

The decision to turn to God in her pain released needed truth to us, and God's presence continued to sustain us through the difficult season. We could also easily see that Joshua was missing out on absolutely nothing! We knew that we had been robbed of having him here on earth to love, but we also knew that we would have eternity in heaven to enjoy him.

As we went through the loss of our son, we began to realize how very much God loved you and I that he sent his Son to earth to die for us. We suddenly understood on a new level what that sacrifice entailed on God the Father's part! As earthly parents, there was no way we would have given Joshua to die for anyone else! But God—that is how much he loved us, his children to be! Our thanksgiving to God for his goodness and lovingkindness deepened during those days.

We still marvel at Father God's heart, which willingly planned to give his Son to pay for the penalty of our sins. How can you not be thankful in face of that demonstration of his love?

EXPERIENCE IS ONLY ONE OF THE TEACHERS

But experience is not the only teacher, just as we have already shared in chapter eight. Reading the Bible is so important because we get to read the testimonies of other people related to God and how he dealt with them as they followed him. It shows us how God has moved in men and for men throughout history, revealing his character and person. God also makes declarations of his purposes and plans that we need to know.

We read in the Old Testament that God was the deliverer for the Israelites, releasing them from their bondage in Egypt. We read that he miraculously provided for them as they wandered in the desert for forty years—water and food as well as shoes that never wore out!

We read about Shadrach, Meshach, and Abed-nego, three men thrown into a very fiery furnace because they would not bow down to the golden image that the king of Babylon, Nebuchadnezzar, had made for his people to worship. The king had been so angry over their disobedience to his command that he made the normal fire in the furnace seven times greater to consume these men. But God—*"the fire had no effect on the bodies of these men nor was the hair of their head singed, nor were their trousers damaged!"* (Daniel 3:8–30)

No wonder the teaching out of the School of the Miraculous at Bethel Church in Redding, California, is encouraging us to see what God will be doing in the end times. They would have us look forward to the birth pangs to see what God will be doing in many instances to prove who he is through his people in signs and wonders and miracles.

We read about Stephen as he was being stoned to death, having an amazing experience. *"But being full of the Holy Spirit, he gazed intently into heaven and saw the glory of God, and Jesus standing at the right hand of God ..."* (Acts 7:55) Many Bible teachers interpret this to mean that he saw Jesus standing to receive him as he departed from this life down here and went to be home with God. As we read this story we see that God will never leave us alone and that although our bodies may perish, we will live forever, welcomed home to be with our God throughout eternity.

Paul said in Philippians 1:21, *"For me, to live is Christ and to die is gain."* He understood, indeed, that Jesus had won the victory over both sin and death. Death was not the victor, but only the door into the fullness of life that is to be experienced in heaven.

It is important to devour the books of the Bible and let them feed you with truth about God, so that your own thanksgiving will increase as you get to know your God better.

AT THE END OF THE AGE

Jesus is very clear in the passages in Matthew and Luke that as we draw near to the end of the age, things are not going to be easy. Jesus lists in both passages a series of extremely difficult things which will begin to happen.

We need to be very careful to be building up our knowledge of God now, every day using our experiences to find God—in every place, as Paul says in 2 Corinthians 2:14. We need to know the Bible and what it says about God so we know him, both the power of the resurrection and also the fellowship of his sufferings. We need to express our thanksgiving for what we are finding out about him day by day.

Thanksgiving will help us keep our heads up and our faces raised to focus on Him during this 'home stretch' of history. It will help us to keep concentrating on the great commission of Jesus and keep our testimony positive and strong as we wait to see our redemption drawing nigh. Thanksgiving is still the most basic expression of our dependence on God and honors Him.

If our loving Father God was able to carry over one million Israelites miraculously through the desert wilderness, He definitely can carry his church through the birth-pang days ahead.

The questions left are: are we going to crumble in fear as the birth pangs begin to come, or are we going to give thanks to God by faith as we see each day unfold?

It may not be easy, but we can set our hearts and minds on a course to keep thanking God as we take each step each day. It will be an adventure worth taking, having the eyes of our heart enlightened to see the hope of our calling (Ephesians 1:18, paraphrased).

CHAPTER 14

IN CONCLUSION

I trust by now it has become clear that the activity of thanksgiving is extremely important. In fact, at this stage in life, I would say that I have learned that God responds to thanksgiving like He does to little else. I think this is because thanksgiving is an indication that our relationship, the Father's and mine, is flowing like it was meant to flow.

As I explained in chapter two, thanksgiving was how I entered into the experience of salvation in Jesus. When I finally said, "Thank you, Jesus, for dying on the cross to be my Savior. Thank you for coming into my life!" I finally began to experience his saving presence.

Thanksgiving was also how I began to experience the presence and work of his Holy Spirit on a whole new level. As I sat in the beautiful Colorado Rockies thanking him for all the beauty I saw around me, the Holy Spirit was released in me in a new way. On a daily basis, I now come before the Holy Spirit and ask him to fill me. Then I thank him for his filling.

The love of the Father has become increasingly real to me as well. My awareness of his love grows and becomes more experiential as I thank him continually for his love for me personally. Although I still love to serve him, I am feeling more and more like a son instead of just a servant.

In fact, I would say that every big step forward in my spiritual life has begun with a thanksgiving which doesn't seem to want to quit. When I think about it, I could say that I have received nothing from the flow of God's goodness and His Kingdom aside from the exercise of thanksgiving, which is the key for me to open the door of faith in God so that I can receive more of his truth and his love.

If you don't know God and his wonders, I encourage you to begin now as I did—by asking him into your life to take his rightful place. Then start thanking Him for saving you and filling you with himself. Please enter into all that he has for you.

I can guarantee you that God will enter in and he will begin to change your life as he has mine—and it is always for the better! You have been designed to have relationship with the Creator God and walk intimately and dependently with him. As you begin to experience his life flowing within you, the flow of thanksgiving will increase and can become as natural as breathing to you.

If you have made it through the book, we want to say a warm "thank you" to you right now. We have shared things in this book that we have shared with no one else about the adventure of our lives.

Our hope is that you have been blessed by this story and have begun to enter into and experience the adventure of a thankful lifestyle for yourself. It will change you and bless those around you.

As you tune your spiritual eyes to see things to thank God for, your knowledge of who he is and what he is doing for you will increase. And soon God will be manifesting through you the "sweet aroma of the knowledge of Him in every place."

I would love to be able to say that after learning about the importance of thanksgiving that I have had no lapses in its flow in me. Unfortunately, it is needless for me to say that there have been times due to busyness and still a few times due to circumstances that have caught me by surprise and thankfulness has been relegated to the background. Sometimes I even just take the flow of things in my life for granted and forget to thank the Father for his good hand upon me.

I am thankful to the Lord, however, for he has again and again brought me back to the simplicity of thankfulness. It has been a big relief to those around me as well, because it is very obvious when I am walking in thanksgiving and when I am not.

For those of you who have read our first book, *The World's Greatest Revivals*, you may remember that we believe there is another major revival with its download of big truth that God means for us to experience. All of us have read or heard teaching that is already in place to support the Bride and the Bridegroom paradigm—which can be read about in Revelation 19:6-7.

I am convinced that one of the most important ways that the Bride makes herself ready for the return of the Bridegroom is by being thankful, on a moment-by-moment basis.

Jesus and the Father are looking for a Bride that is eager for his return, a Bride who is responding to his love and care for her. Thanksgiving is the best and most appropriate response to all that Jesus has done for us—and is doing for us—on a daily basis.

THANK YOU, FATHER! THANK YOU, JESUS! THANK YOU, HOLY SPIRIT! THANK YOU FOR ALL YOU ARE DOING TO GET US READY FOR THE CULMINATION OF THE AGES, EVERYTHING BEING WRAPPED UP IN JESUS AND PRESENTED TO THE FATHER. THANK YOU THAT YOU HAVE GOOD PLANS FOR US ALL AND THAT YOU ARE LEADING US IN YOUR TRIUMPH.

THANKSGIVING
AS A NATIONAL HOLIDAY

I have a university degree in history and often look at things through an historic lens. I wonder sometimes if the study of history should not teach us something so that we don't repeat the same mistakes over and over again each century. As I began to think about thanksgiving and its fruit, my history lens went into high gear.

THE JUDEO HERITAGE OF THANKSGIVING

Prayers of thanksgiving and special feast days for the giving of thanks to God, the Creator of heaven and earth, are part and parcel of Old Testament practice and history. Israel, His people, honored and acknowledged him as God, their provider, guide, and friend. Feast days were celebrated even before God Himself instituted the *official* feast days for Israel.

The feast days were times of thanksgiving as they commemorated things God had done for them. Some were pictures of things still to happen. Passover, one of those feast days they celebrated each year, was both a commemoration of how God had delivered them from their slavery in Egypt and a picture of Jesus as the Lamb of God who was coming in the future to die for the salvation of humanity.

Israel's feast days were commemorated with the whole nation coming together, setting aside time to remember his unfailing love and provision for them. These became cultural as well as religious observances and were passed on into the Christian era after Jesus' death and resurrection.

THE CHRISTIAN HERITAGE OF THANKSGIVING

In James W. Baker's book, *Thanksgiving: the Biography of an American Holiday*, pages 1–14, there are many interesting facts about official and unofficial thanksgiving as it developed after the advent of Christ. Here are just a few:

As Christianity grew in influence, enough to be recognized by Constantine as the religion of the Roman Empire, the Pope, as the recognized leader of Christianity, built upon this tradition of religious feast days. Soon there were 95 church holidays on the Catholic calendar as well as the 52 Sundays a year upon which the people were required to attend church and forego work. At times they were even called upon to pay for the expensive celebrations. By the time the Reformation took place, the people were glad to see the long list of calendared events reduced to only 27 church holidays.

Some groups, like the radical Puritan reformers, wanted to eliminate all church holidays, including Christmas and Easter. They wanted to replace the former with Days of Fasting or Days of Thanksgiving. The Puritans felt that Days of Fasting were to be called when unexpected disasters, which they interpreted as threats of judgment from on high, loomed on the horizon like the drought in 1611, the floods in 1613, and the plagues in both 1604 and 1622.

Days of Thanksgiving were called following the victory of England over the Spanish Armada in 1588 and the deliverance of Queen Anne in 1705. The Days of Fasting and Days of

Thanksgiving travelled with the Puritans and the Pilgrims to North America when they emigrated from England.

The many other immigrants to North America from Sweden, Ireland, Holland, France, and England, to mention a few, also brought to the New World their traditions of giving thanks to God for abundant harvests. This feasting together was done within communities after the hard work of harvesting was over.

When these traditions were combined in the New World with the indigenous peoples who helped the newcomers survive their first winters, introducing new plants and agricultural processes, the stage was set in North America for the two emerging North American nations to institute national holidays of thanksgiving to the God of the Bible. We will take a brief look now at what happened in Canada and the United States, two countries that have instituted a recognized, national holiday of thanksgiving that originally was directed to the God of the Bible.

ROOTS OF THANKSGIVING IN CANADA

Dorothy Duncan has written an interesting book called *Feasting and Fasting: Canada's Heritage Celebrations* in which she explains that long before the arrival of newcomers, the First Nations peoples were giving thanks to their Sacred Mother for the fall harvest each year as it was gathered, prepared, and stored for the long winters that followed (p. 238). Then the settlers came from around the world to Canada with their memories and traditions from their homelands of the informal thanksgiving services and meals which also surrounded the fall harvesting season each year.

Coming to a new land was full of surprises, with new flora

and fauna to explore. Some of the foods they were used to didn't grow in North America, and without the help from the First Nations peoples already in the land, the European settlers might not have survived at all. The First Nations peoples taught the new settlers not only which of the plants in North America were edible but also taught them their indigenous agricultural tricks. So in the early years thanksgiving after an arduous harvest season was natural as the new settlers thanked both God and their neighbors for their survival.

In Canada a thanksgiving feast day is recorded surrounding the survival of the explorer Martin Frobisher who had been trying to find a northern passage to the Pacific Ocean. His thanksgiving celebration was not over a harvest, but was thanksgiving for surviving the long journey from Europe through perils of storms and icebergs. In 1578, on his third and final voyage to this area, he held a formal ceremony in Frobisher Bay on Baffin Island to give thanks to God (p. 239). This tradition of a feast would continue as more settlers began to arrive in the Canadian colonies.

One of the informal Canadian Thanksgiving Days was decreed by Queen Victoria on April 15, 1872. She proclaimed this day to be one of thanksgiving for the nation to celebrate the Prince of Wales' recovery from a serious illness (p. 241).

From the many informal thanksgiving days celebrated after fall harvests or decreed by royalty, the Province of Canada created the nation's first Thanksgiving Day in 1859, asking all Canadians to spend the holiday in "public and solemn" recognition of God's mercies (p. 241). Then on October 9, 1879, the Marquis of Lorne, then governor general, proclaimed a statutory holiday on November 6 as "a day of General Thanksgiving to Almighty God for the bountiful harvest with which Canada has been blessed" (p. 241).

Finally, in 1957, the Canadian Parliament passed legislation making this same Thanksgiving Day an annual holiday to be celebrated on the second Monday of October every year (p. 242) It is a statutory holiday in all provinces except New Brunswick and Nova Scotia and stores are closed in all but those two provinces on that day.

ROOTS OF THANKSGIVING IN
THE UNITED STATES OF AMERICA

In *Festivals Together, A Guide to Multi-Cultural Celebration*, there is a short history of the famous first thanksgiving feast held by the immigrants who arrived on the shores of what later became known as the United States. Just like the history of Canada, many Europeans settlers came due to religious persecution, and they were seeking freedom to worship God according to the ways he had revealed to them.

They came with little more than the clothes they had on their backs. Many had had to sell their homes, businesses, and farms just to buy passage to The New World. After the dangerous voyage over the Atlantic, many were barely alive due to illness stemming from the over-crowded conditions on the ships that brought them.

They sought and found opportunity for a new start in the new land. During their first year, they almost didn't survive as they waited for crops to be harvested from soil that they weren't yet familiar with. But survive they did and they were able to worship God with freedom in their own unique ways.

The traditional story celebrated in school plays around Thanksgiving Day in the US is about the Pilgrims in Plymouth, present day Massachusetts, in 1621 (p. 143). Their response to their survival was thanksgiving to God for His supply, mercy, and grace during those first months. They invited the native people to participate with them since the were to ones who helped teach them how to cultivate crops that made their harvest possible. They celebrated this feast for a week the first year, according to Barbara Greenwood in her book, *A Pioneer Thanksgiving* (p. 47). They then established a feast day every year called "Thanksgiving Day."

In 1789 George Washington, the first U.S. President, issued a Thanksgiving proclamation, but people were free to decide for themselves whether or not they wanted to celebrate. Gradually, most communities chose one fall Sunday to decorate the church with the fruits of the harvest.

In the 1850's a magazine editor, Sarah Hall, began writing about Thanksgiving, and the idea for an official annual holiday caught on (p. 47).

President Abraham Lincoln made a presidential proclamation in 1863 that named the last Thursday of November Thanksgiving Day. Even then, not everyone celebrated (p. 47). Some people feel that Lincoln's hope was that such a national holiday would help unify the Northern and the Southern states after the Civil War which had nearly torn the country apart.

Finally, a Congressional proclamation made during the presidency of Franklin D. Roosevelt in December of 1941 set the date of this national holiday so that it is now held on the fourth Thursday of November each year. Upon this Congressional proclamation, Thanksgiving Day became an official national holiday in the United States.

MY OBSERVATIONS

I haven't travelled to every country in the world, but in those forty-five countries I have visited, I have asked if they have an official national day of thanksgiving that acknowledges God's goodness. It would appear that only Canada and the United States have set aside official days off from work and study to celebrate thanksgiving as families feast together. It is no longer a feast following marginal survival, however, and in many cases Father God no longer is thanked as profusely for His provision and blessings, as our countries have become increasingly secularized. But the history is there and lies underneath it all.

I do not think that it is an accident that these nations have grown in prominence, even over those from which they came. Blessing is the response from our loving Father God who receives their thanksgiving.

With that in mind, I hope that the citizens of the United States and Canada will not stray far from their roots where thanksgiving flowed *officially to God*. We can see on many levels how the reduction of Thanksgiving Day to "turkey day" is just another one of the secularizing trends to back away from God as our Provider and the One on whom we rely. I believe that this is a short sighted and dangerous trend. God is always quick to bless and slow to remove blessing, but I realize that God could begin to remove the level of blessing that we in North America have come to enjoy and expect—if we continue to move away from our roots of acknowledging our dependence upon him through thanksgiving to him for all that he provides for us, individually and corporately.

In my estimation, lack of thankfulness is also dangerous for a society because the result can be that self-aggrandizing pride in our own accomplishments and conceit will creep in to take its place.

WORKS CITED

A Pioneer Thanksgiving, Barbara Greenwood. Kids Can Press, Toronto, Canada, 1999.

Feasting and Fasting: Canada's Heritage Celebrations, Dorothy Duncan. Dundurn Press, Toronto, Canada, 2010.

Festivals Together, Sue Fitzjohn, Minda Weston, Judy Large. Hawthorne Press, Stroud, Glouchestershire, UK, 1993.

Thanksgiving: the Biography of an American Holiday, Baker, James W., University Press of New Hampshire, 2009.

YOU WERE MADE FOR MORE

A God who
loves you

wants you to
experience him

be transformed

and given
power

At Catch The Fire, we are passionate about seeing people be transformed by a living God. We have many books that can help you on your journey, but we are also involved in much more.

Why not join us at a conference or seminar this year? Or come on a short-term mission with us? Or have your heart radically changed at a 5-month school. Or just visit one of our churches in many cities around the world.

CONTINUE YOUR JOURNEY AT

catchthefirebooks.com/whatsnext

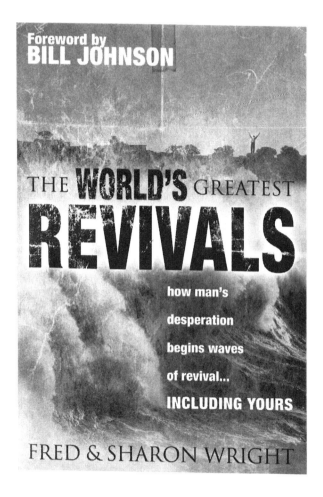

Foreword by
BILL JOHNSON

THE WORLD'S GREATEST

REVIVALS

how man's
desperation
begins waves
of revival...
INCLUDING YOURS

FRED & SHARON WRIGHT

THE WORLD'S GREATEST REVIVALS

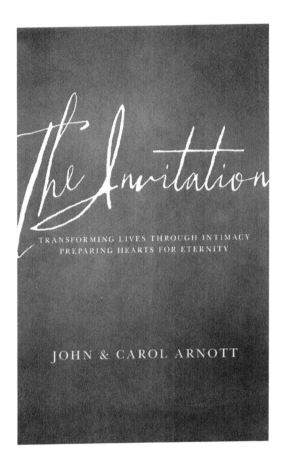

THE INVITATION
JOHN & CAROL ARNOTT

CATCH THE FIRE BOOKS

CONSUMED BY LOVE

DUNCAN SMITH

ABOUT THE AUTHORS

Fred and Sharon Wright both met the Lord at the age of 19 while attending different universities in separate locations. Then they were both separately led to England to attend the Capernwray Bible School near Carnforth, England and there they met each other for the first time in 1962. God used this Bible course, which lasted for six months, to ground them each in their faith and prepare them for their life together as man and wife.

God led them together at the end of the Bible School and, at the last minute, gave them a joint assignment. They were asked to accompany and help Christian Bastke, one of their teachers at the Bible School, in an evangelistic youth conference in West Berlin, Germany. This was their beginning to their life-long focus of serving God together.

During the two years that it took to complete their university degrees, Fred served Youth for Christ in the Los Angeles area, being responsible for 15 of their evangelistic clubs, which were meeting on high school campuses in the San Fernando Valley. In 1965, after receiving their BA's at what is now Azusa Pacific University, they moved to Denver, Colorado. There, Fred completed his Masters of Divinity Degree at Denver Seminary in 1968. During this time they worked with youth in a local church.

In 1968, after Fred's graduation from seminary, they took on the position of Associate Pastor in Seaside, California, for

18 months. Then, in April of 1970, they left for the country of Sweden to work in missions there for eleven years. During their years in Sweden, the heyday of the Jesus People Movement of the 1970's broke out. It was an exciting decade with over 4,000,000 young people coming to the Lord out of the hippy culture worldwide.

To accommodate the needs of this era, Fred and Sharon founded the Capernwray Bible School and Conference Center in Holsby Brunn in the southern part of Sweden. Well over 1,000 students came through the school during their tenure there. Many of these students continue serving Christ's Body in leadership on mission fields or in the pastorate in many different countries around the world.

Upon returning from Sweden in 1981, they served in three different churches, two of which they planted, the second growing to well over five hundred people.

In 1996 God led them to Toronto, Ontario, Canada where they helped plant and pastor the network of churches known as Partners in Harvest, which was born out of the Toronto Blessing move of God beginning in January of 1994. There are now well over 13,000 churches in this network worldwide, thanks in part to the ever-expanding work of Heidi and Rolland Baker's ministry, IRIS, in Mozambique.

The list of Fred and Sharon's mentors and fathers in the faith include Jack Hamilton and Bob Crane of Youth For Christ, Ray Steadman of Peninsula Bible Church near Palo Alto, California, Vernon Grounds, President of Denver Seminary, Major Ian Thomas of Capernwray Missionary Fellowship, Roger Forster of Ichthus Christian Fellowship of the house church movement in England, John Wimber of the Vineyard movement, John Arnott of Catch The Fire movement, Bill Johnson of Bethel Church, Redding, California, and Jack Winter, James Jordan and Jack Frost of the Father Heart movement. They both feel so thankful to have been exposed to such a diverse group of leaders in the Body of Christ and to glean from such a wide spectrum of Bible teaching.

Fred and Sharon have the privilege of carrying several important messages to the Body of Christ around the world. Fred has travelled well over 1,000,000 miles already, speaking on the Infilling and Indwelling Life of Christ, on Father God's Love for His children, on the Importance of Living in the Fullness of the Holy Spirit, and on the Preparation for the Return of Jesus Christ for His Bride.

Fred and Sharon are published authors of the highly-regarded book, *The World's Greatest Revivals*.

They also serve on the leadership team of River Community Church, Abbotsford, British Columbia between ministry trips and trips back to Ontario, Canada where they love to visit their three precious grandchildren, wonderful gifts from their daughter, Hanna Lafferty and her husband, Mark Lafferty. Fred and Sharon also have an amazing entrepreneurial son, Nathan Wright, who is growing his own business in Japan. His wife, Megumi works for a Japanese pharmaceutical company a train ride away from their home.